WILDLIFE TRAFFICKING
A Crime against Environmet

Siddhartha Sarkar

GYAN

Published, 2019

Published by

Gyan Publishing House
5, Ansari Road
Daryaganj, New Delhi-110002
Phone: 011-47034999, 9811692060
www.gyanbooks.com
E-mail: books@gyanbooks.com

Printed at: G. Print Process, Delhi.

Cataloging in Publication Data—DK
Courtesy: D.K. Agencies (P) Ltd. <docinfo@dkagencies.com>

Wildlife trafficking : a crime against environment / [edited by], Dr. Siddhartha Sarkar.
pages cm
Contributed articles.
ISBN 9788121219648

1. Wild animal trade. 2. Wildlife smuggling. I. Sarkar, Siddhartha, editor.

LCC SK591.W55 2018 | DDC 333.954 23

Contents

Preface

Wildlife trafficking is a major part of underground economy, and the largest global illegal trade after drug trafficking. Illegal wildlife trade is driven mainly by the huge profits earned by the traffickers with comparatively low risk and low penalties make the trade highly lucrative. Unlike other conventional crimes, no stigma is attached to the offenders who commit wildlife crimes. During the past decade, wildlife trafficking, the poaching or other taking of protected or managed species and the illegal trade in wildlife and their related parts and products, has escalated into an international crisis. Each year, hundreds of millions of plants and animals are caught or harvested from the wild and then sold as food, pets, ornamental plants, leather, tourist curios, and medicine whereas a great deal of this trading is operated illegally threatening the survival of many endangered species.

Providing a global assessment of wildlife crime is challenging, because every country protects its animals, fish, timber, and other plant life in different ways. There are international instruments defining other forms of organised crime, including drug trafficking, human trafficking, firearms trafficking, and smuggling of migrants. But there is no equivalent agreement defining wildlife crime, so there is no universally accepted definition of the term. This is not to say that wildlife is unprotected internationally. The *Convention on International Trade in Endangered Species of Wild Fauna and Flora*, known as CITES, provides a framework to protect and regulate international trade in certain species. It does not define wildlife crime as such, but it strongly influences national legislation on wildlife crime, and provides a means for cooperation against trafficking. Parties to CITES are required to 'penalise' illegal trade. It is an agreement of remarkable power and scope. CITES is so important because most wildlife protection laws are situated in broader national environmental legislation. As a result, these laws naturally focus on domestic species, and they do so in a wide variety of ways. Since wildlife populations are dynamic, most wildlife protection laws leave it to the executive branch of the government to issue regulations determining when and how wildlife can be harvested. Species can be added and removed from protected species lists, licenses issued allowing the legal taking of wildlife, and quotas established to ensure sustainability. As a result, the domestic legality of any given wildlife product is a matter of considerable complexity.

The real problem comes when wildlife, not listed under CITES, is taken illegally in one country and transported to another. The protected species lists of most countries are limited to domestic species, and there may be no basis in national law to challenge the import or sale of questionable wildlife products. Even if the law allows the seizure of wildlife taken or exported contrary to the laws and regulations of other countries, proving this illegality can be challenging. Few countries have the capacity to keep track of the complex and changing world of foreign wildlife regulation, or to gather evidence on offences committed on the other side of the world. This is where CITES comes in. It allows countries to reciprocally protect one another's species according to a common set of rules. The system works through a series of permits and certificates relating to three international protected species lists, the CITES appendices. International trade in CITES-listed wildlife without the appropriate permits and certificates appears to be the most commonly detected transnational wildlife crime.

As with other illicit economies, evaluating the effectiveness of policy measures is difficult. The lack of baselines and insufficient data compound the difficulties, and establishing causality for complex ecological and social phenomena is a complicated undertaking. Often, there is enormous uncertainty regarding the species status and population trends, the size of legal and illegal exploitation, the exact locale-specific drivers of harvesters, the causes of decline of a species and the relative importance of the trade – as opposed, for example – to habitat degradation, for example, the definition and level of sustainable exploitation, and the interactive dynamics among these factors. It is thus imperative to tailor policies to particular local cultural and institutional settings as well as to particular ecological needs of particular species in particular locales. That of course implies that effective regulation requires an enormous amount of case-specificity and imposes great demands on local data generation and monitoring over time.

However, this study is designed to explain the basic structure of organised criminal group, their modus operandi and trade route; the prevalence of, and drivers leading to, wildlife trafficking; global treaties and agreements, and the efforts of the non-governmental organisations to influence the wildlife protection policy agenda.

Siddhartha Sarkar

1

Wildlife Trafficking: A Concept Analysis

Siddhartha Sarkar, A.C.College of Commerce, India

Introduction

The term 'wild life' was first used by the famous American Zoologist William Temple Hornaday in his book 'Our Vanishing Wild Life (Its Extermination and Preservation)' published in 1913. It was only in 1930s that 'wildlife', written as a single word, came into widespread usage. Wildlife means the native wild fauna and flora of a region. As per Section 2(37) of the Wild Life (Protection) Act, 1972, 'wildlife' includes any animal, aquatic or land vegetation which forms part of any habitat.

Importance of wildlife is to be seen in the light of the constitutional mandate. (Protection) and improvement of environment and safeguarding of forests and wildlife is included in the Directive Principles of State Policy in the Constitution of India (Article 48 A). Article 51A (g) of the Constitution says that it is the Fundamental Duty of every citizen to protect and improve the natural environment including forests, lakes, rivers and wildlife, and to have compassion for living creatures. Prevention of cruelty to animals, Forests and (Protection) of wild animals and birds are in the Concurrent List, (List -III), Seventh Schedule under Article 246 of the Constitution of India.

Wildlife crime can be defined as taking, possession, trade or movement, processing, consumption of wild animals and plants or their derivatives in contravention of any international, regional, or national legislation(s). Infliction of cruelty to and the persecution of wild animals, both free-living and captive are also at times added to this definition. Though wild animals and plants are the victims of any wildlife crime at first place, it has got a cascading effect on the ecosystem of particular country or region. It is clear from the constitutional mandate that wildlife is our national wealth. Therefore, the country is also a victim of wildlife crimes. As illegal wildlife trade involves huge amounts of money, it is, also to be treated as a serious economic offence.

Hunting and illegal trade are the major wildlife offences. All other offences like preparation, possession, transportation, processing etc are ancillary offences. That being so, wildlife offenders can be divided into two groups – (a) the poachers or hunters who kill or capture wild animals or collect wild plants, and (b) persons buying hunted and/or captured animals or its body parts or derivatives or collected plants or its parts or derivatives, for own consumption or for trade. The traders of wildlife materials constitute the most influential group of wildlife offenders and they operate in highly organized manner. Networks of such organized wildlife criminals have global presence and they make maximum commercial gain from these crimes.

Poaching is often associated with different levels of violence. Poaching for ivory, Rhino horns etc. are traditionally based on heavy use of weaponry which may eventually bring even human bloodshed. Whereas, poaching of other species like Snakes, Orchids, Turtles etc. are more dependent on technical skills to recognize high-value species. In Indian context, the poachers are often compelled by the poor socio-economic conditions.

Wildlife crimes are often interconnected to other crime forms like murder, theft, drugs etc., but differ in following aspects:

(i) Wildlife crimes are location specific. To commit a wildlife crime, the offender has to invariably go to the place where the targeted wildlife is available.

(ii) Acts which are now construed as a wildlife offences were not criminal acts until enactment of the Wild Life (Protection) Act, 1972. Hunting, that tops the list of wildlife crimes, was once an act of valour and a royal pass time. The great hunters used to be the heroes of their times.

(iii) Public at large is not affected or disturbed by the wildlife crimes. In the case of conventional crimes like murder, theft or robbery, every incident infuses a sense of fear into the minds of people that anybody could be a victim of such criminal acts and public at large is concerned about such activities and contribute towards prevention of such crimes. This does not happen in case of wildlife crimes.

In 2003 the United Nations Office on Drugs and Crime (UNODC) included wildlife crimes in the list of Transnational Organized Crimes (TOC). Transnational Organized Crime, as defined by the UNODC is 'a structured group of three or more persons, acting together with the aim of committing one or more serious crime, in order to obtain financial or material benefit and these crimes are planned and/or committed in more than one country'. A serious crime is an offence punishable by an imprisonment of at least 4 years or more. Therefore, most of the wildlife crimes fall in the category of serious crimes.

Illegal wildlife trade is driven mainly by the huge profits earned by the traders. Low risk and low penalties make the trade highly lucrative. Unlike other conventional crimes, no stigma is attached to the offenders who commit wildlife crimes. Wealthy markets in Asia, Europe, USA and the Middle East are the force driving the illegal trade of wildlife. Craze for ornaments made of animal body parts (ivory, tiger teeth/bones), use of animal body parts or plants in traditional medicines, keeping the skins or horns or antlers as status symbols, cultural beliefs or even superstitious beliefs are other factors driving the illegal trade in wildlife and their parts and products.

Illegal trade is by definition a hidden activity. As such it is almost impossible to obtain reliable figures, but it is estimated that the total value of illegal wildlife trade runs into billions of dollars. Wildlife trafficking has been defined as 'any environment-related crime that involves the illegal trade, smuggling, poaching, capture or collection of endangered species, protected wildlife (including animals and plants that are subject to harvest quotas and regulated by permits), derivatives, or products thereof'. It includes all sales or exchanges of wild animal and plant resources by illegal means. Under the Convention on International Trade in Endangered Species of Wild Fauna and Flora (CITES), to which governments voluntarily adhere, only trade that does not threaten the survival of a species is permitted. Southeast Asia, with its linkages into the larger Asian market that includes China, Indonesia, and India, is one of the world's 'wildlife trade hotspots', a region where unsustainable and ill regulated trade in wildlife poses a disproportionally large threat to biodiversity and species preservation (Davis, 2005). Both the volume and diversity of traded and consumed species have increased to phenomenal and unprecedented levels. Wildlife is being extracted from Southeast Asia's tropical forests at many times the sustainable rate (Bennett, 2002), with the illegal wildlife trade there estimated to be worth $8 to $10 billion per year (Lovgren, 2008). Based on data through the 2000s, scientists expect that between 13 and 42 percent of Southeast Asia's animal and plant species could be wiped out during this century. At least half of those losses would represent global extinctions (ASEAN-WEN, 2009).

As with all illicit economies, estimating the size of the illegal trade in wildlife is inherently difficult because much of the trade is clandestine, hidden, and often minimally monitored. Moreover, unlike in the case of the illegal trade in drugs, for example, no regular monitoring mechanisms exist to monitor either wildlife populations throughout the world or the size of the illegal trade in wildlife globally and in specific regions. Often only NGO monitoring, such as by TRAFFIC, or sporadic scientific studies provide data on wildlife population levels for particular species or the size of the illegal trade. Thus only limited data are often available, time series studies and trends are lacking, and the only available information on the size of a particular species population or the illegal trade in it may be a decade or two old.

Nonetheless, even with highly imperfect data that vastly underestimates the size of illegal trade in wildlife, the amount of wildlife removed from forests and waters of Southeast Asia and traded there and globally is shocking. It is estimated that between 1998 and 2007 over 35 million CITES-listed animals (0.3 million butterflies; 16.0 million seahorses; 0.1 million other fish, 17.4 million reptiles; 0.4 million mammals; and 1.0 million birds) were exported. Out of these, 30 million (approximately 300 species) were wild-caught while the remaining 4.5 million were derived from captive breeding programs. In addition, 18 million pieces and 2 million kg of live corals were exported (Nijman, 2010). Out of the total exports, the proportion of illegal to legal trade in wildlife was relatively low, involving less than a quarter of a million individuals of species over the decade (Robinson, 2002). However, since these numbers were obtained from official documents governing the trade in CITES listed species, and thus represents mainly legal trade and seizures of illegally-traded items; the number is probably only a fraction of the actual trade in wildlife throughout Asia, much of which is undocumented and illegal. For example, Sabine Schoppe estimated that in the 1990s and 2000s, some 2 million box turtles were exported from Indonesia annually, greatly exceeding the official Indonesian quota of 18,000 (Schoppe, 2009) ; hence more than 99 percent of the trade in box turtles from Indonesia was illegal. Similarly, Chris Sheperd showed that in 1999 and 2000, 25 tons of wild freshwater turtles and tortoises were caught and exported each week from northern Sumatra to China, amounting to about 1300 tons a year just from one small region (Sheperd, 2000). It is estimated that trade in Tockay gecko from Java amounted to some 1.2 million individuals a year, enormously exceeding the Indonesian quota of 25,000

(Schoppe, 2009), and implying that 98 percent of the trade was illegal. Overall, over 50 percent of Asia's freshwater turtles (45 species) are now considered in danger of extinction as a result of overexploitation (Peter Paul Van Dijk, 2000). Almost 30,000 items made from the critically endangered marine hawksbill turtle were found on sale in Vietnam in 2002, signifying the death of thousands of the turtles (TRAFFIC-Southeast Asia Indochina, 2004). Overall, among reptiles, the most commonly traded species from Southeast Asia are soft-shell turtles, box turtles, cobras, pythons, monitors, and crocodiles. In critically endangered species, the numbers of killed animals are far smaller, but the detrimental effects on species survival are often even greater. Feeding the strong Chinese market, 51 tigers, for example, were illegally killed in Sumatra between 1998 and 2002, out of a population of around 800 individuals before 1998. In north-eastern Laos, 7 tigers were killed during 2003 and 2004, and their bones sold for about $50,000. A shocking 2,200 tigers are estimated to have been killed by poachers in India in the last decade, crashing its population by two thirds, with only between 1,000 and 3,000 tigers left today, and critically threatening three decades of tiger conservation efforts (Srivastava, 2010).

Measuring Illicit Trade

Illegal wildlife trade in simple terms refers to sale or exchange of wild animals or plant resources, trade of which is prohibited under the law. This may involve live or dead animals or plants and their derivatives. The trade may be for the pet or horticultural trades, or trade in wild animal and plant products such as skins, medicinal ingredients, tourist curios, timber, wild meat and other food products sought after by humans. Due to the clandestine nature of the illegal wildlife trade, it is very difficult to estimate its exact value. Interpol has stated on its website that various governmental and non-governmental agencies have estimated that the value of the illegal wildlife trade may be in excess of USD 20 billion annually. The United States of America's State Department estimates that the market value of illegal wildlife products has reached USD 10 billion a year and possibly twice that. The actual figure may never be known, as much of the trade occurs in less developed parts of the world, but could in fact be significantly higher (Sinha, 2010).

Illicit wildlife trafficking has increased over the last few years despite the combined efforts of the international community, governments and civil society. The trend is confirmed by some of the most recent events relating to wildlife trafficking. For example, 2011 was the highest year on record for elephant poaching; the theft of rhinoceros horns from museums, auction houses and antique shops has increased in the European Union; ivory estimated to weigh more than 23 tons – a figure that represents 2,500 elephants – was confiscated in 17 large-scale (>800 kg) seizures of illegal ivory in 2011; and the illegal poaching of rhinos in South Africa surged to a record high in 2011, with a final death toll of 448 (Department of Environmental Affairs, Republic of South Africa, 2012).

The trade has become a lucrative business for criminal syndicates. The risk involved is low compared to drug trafficking, and high profits can be generated. The price of rhinoceros horn has increased to around US$60,000 per kilogram – twice the value of gold and platinum – and it is now more valuable on the black market than diamonds and cocaine (Neo, 2009). The penalties associated with trafficking rhinoceros horn are not aligned to its value: poachers convicted under the North West Province law in South Africa may get away with a US$14,000 fine, while trafficking up to 5 grams of cocaine is sentenced with not less than five years in jail (Michler, 2011). The situation is no different in demand countries, where those found to be in possession of drugs are far more seriously punished than those in the possession of illegal wildlife products.

The rise in Asian demand for trafficked wildlife can be linked directly to poaching increases in Africa, as shown by the CITES elephant report to the 62nd Standing Committee meeting. This document reports, for example, that elephant poaching increases in Africa are closely correlated with increases in consumer purchasing power in China, the main demand country for ivory (CITES, 2012).

In wildlife trade, both legal and illegal, there is always a value chain from the capture or harvesting of wildlife to transportation and marketing to consumers. Intermediate collation and/or processing destinations are usually found along the chain. In this general pattern, a distinction can be made between source countries and consumer countries, but the two roles are not necessarily mutually exclusive. Organized criminal groups essentially form distribution networks across national boundaries linking source countries and consumer countries, often via important transit destinations.

In many cases, illegal wildlife trade has led to over-exploitation of the targeted species, to the point where the very survival of these species is becoming difficult. This aspect has been well publicized in the case of Tigers, rhinos, elephants, Star Tortoises and others. Over harvesting for trade has also affected populations of many freshwater and marine species such as otters, freshwater and marine turtles, corals, sharks, tuna and other sea fish.

Furthermore, illegal wildlife trade indirectly threatens the livelihoods of a large part of our human population who are dependent on wildlife products from forest and coastal biomes to sustain them. These inhabitants not only depend on the resources from the wild for food but also for their livelihood and healthcare. It is therefore crucial that these wildlife resources are managed sustainably and conserved according to the law.

The primary motivating factor for wildlife traders is economic, ranging from efforts to secure basic survival and everyday livelihoods, via small scale local income generation to a major profit-oriented business, such as marine fisheries and logging companies. Between collectors of wildlife and the ultimate users, any number of middlemen may be involved in wildlife trade, including specialists involved in storage, handling, transport, taxidermy and preservation, manufacturing, processing and extraction, industrial production, marketing, and the export and retail businesses. In fact, most of us are involved in wildlife trade in some way, even if just as end consumers of wildlife products of flora and fauna.

In India, trade in wildlife resources has always been pivotal in the livelihoods of a large number of people especially the tribal. Communities living around forest areas have been dependent on natural resources for their survival. They have engaged in trade of forest produce either for cash or on a barter system to be able to meet their household requirements. However, such trade was mostly sustainable and did not severely impact the survival of the plant and animal species.

Driven by an overall human population increase and related consumer demand, including 'modernized' collection, harvesting and transport means, the need within people involved in the trade has become commercialized and, when illegal, has evolved into a well organised clandestine operation. At the source of the operation are the harvesters, collectors or poachers who often reside in rural areas without direct access to channels of distribution. They rely on visiting buyers to market their goods. In addition, there are numerous middlemen who run a well organised nexus to transport and market illegal wildlife products.

A large part of this trade is meant for the international market and has no direct demand in India. Some examples are the Tiger, otter and Leopard skins that are used to make *chubas* (traditional robes worn by Tibetans); Tiger, Rhino and Musk Deer body parts and derivatives meant for use in traditional Chinese medicines and rhino horns used to make dagger handles in countries like Yemen etc.

There is a huge trade in wildlife goods world-wide, with China being the largest market followed by significant markets in the United States of America and the European Union. Trade is both international and domestic, with large volumes of the latter particularly within developing nations. The European Union (EU) tops the list of major importer by value for many wild animal and plant products, including tropical timber, caviar, reptile skins and live reptiles. The legal trade of wildlife products into the EU alone was worth an estimated EUR 93 billion in 2005. The value of legal global international wildlife trade, including non-CITES species and based on declared import values in 2005, is conservatively estimated to be about EUR 249 billion per year, with timber and fisheries accounting for about 90% of this value. As a comparison, the UN Statistics Division records the declared import value of the global trade in coffee, tea, and spices in 2005 at about EUR 14 billion, while domestic sales of medicinal plants in China was valued at around EUR 19 billion in 2002, and has increased by 8% a year since 1994 (Engler and Parry-Jones, 2007).

Wildlife trade involves hundreds of millions of individual plants and animals from tens of thousands of species. Timber and seafood are the most important categories of international wildlife trade, in terms of both volume and value. According to the United Nations Food and Agriculture Organisation (FAO), more than 100 million tons of fish were traded in 1998, and more than a billion cubic meters of wood products were exported globally in 1999 (IUCN and Accor, 2008).

TRAFFIC estimates that from 2000-2005, 3.4 million lizard skins, 2.9 million crocodile skins and 3.4 million snake skins, all species listed under CITES, were imported into the EU, along with 300000 live snakes for the pet trade. In 2004 alone, the EU imported more than 10 million cubic meters of tropical timber from Africa, South America and Asia, worth USD 1.9 billion. In 1996, global international trade in medicinal and aromatic plants amounted to more than 440,000 tons (Engler and Parry-Jones, 2007).

International trade in species of conservation concern is regulated by CITES. From 1995 to 1999, CITES recorded an annual average of more than 1.5 million live birds, 640,000 live reptiles, 300,000 crocodilian skins, 1.6 million lizard skins, 1.1 million snake skins, 150,000 furs, almost 300 tons of caviar, more than 1 million coral pieces and 21,000 hunting trophies (IUCN and Accor, 2008).

The international supply chain for illicit wildlife trafficking involves organized criminal groups that are attracted to the availability of huge profits and the low-risk nature of the crime, including the absence of credible enforcement, prosecution, penalties and other deterrents. The profits to be made are very high, with the value of the products increasing by multiples of 25 to 50 along the commodity chain (Brack and Hayman, 2002). There are many different actors who facilitate the supply side of illicit wildlife trafficking. Illegal wildlife products are generated in a range of different ways – from local individual poachers who, facilitated by local middlemen, act out of opportunism or need; to criminal and rebel groups that seek to finance their illegal activities; and professional international hunters who use their experience for higher profit, often working for international clients. Illegal wildlife products can also come from legally hunted trophies, privately held stocks not declared or registered with the authorities, or the theft of products from private and public owners and institutions.

International Law and Regulation

International legislation refers to global treaties (or conventions) and agreements that are open to participation by all nations. The CITES Convention applies specifically to the subject. Just over 150 countries have either signed or ratified CITES, the prime purpose of which is to regulate trade in the species listed in its Appendices, either by outright prohibition or by monitoring trade levels. The Convention on Biological Diversity (CBD, or Biodiversity Convention) encourages parties to protect the biological diversity in their countries through a variety of mechanisms. They are also encouraged to manage and reap benefits from their genetic resources that are in demand from other countries (22, 28, 42). In a number of circumstances, this has led to curbs on, or careful regulation of, the international movement of genetic material, thus affecting trade in certain species, particularly non-human primates, and to sensitivity about the export of tissue samples for commercial purposes. The Convention or, more specifically, national legislation designed to control the exploitation of genetic resources may therefore impinge upon international wildlife trade in certain circumstances. The WTO has the overarching responsibility for regulating international trade, including the trade in wildlife (48). For the purposes of this chapter, it is important to focus on the Agreement on the Application of Sanitary and Phytosanitary Measures (SPS Agreement), since this text provides common principles on which national animal health laws must be based for the purpose of international trade. This Agreement, ratified in 1995, clearly states that import measures cannot be discriminatory, or constitute unjustified trade barriers, must be based on science and conducted with transparency. For the purpose of animal health and zoonoses it recognizes the OIE as the relevant organisation which sets the standards for terrestrial and aquatic animal health and zoonoses upon which countries have to base their import measures (34, 35, 36, 37).

There is no mechanism in the CITES for the enforcement of its provisions other than at national level. Likewise, the animal health and welfare laws have to be enforced by using the judicial systems of individual countries. In addition, in respect of animal health, the WTO requires the OIE standards and recommendations to be upheld in accordance with the provisions of the WTO SPS Agreement. The WTO provides a mechanism for the resolution of trade disputes relating to this Agreement.

The CITES is a global treaty, membership of which is available to all governments of the world (9). The Convention was opened for signature in 1973 and entered into force on 1st July 1975. By December 2001, there were 155 countries that had become party to the Convention (also known as the Washington Convention, from the place where the Convention was concluded, but is commonly referred to as 'CITES'). The Convention applies to situations in which CITES-listed species are moved across international boundaries. While animals remain within the territory of a country, trade or movement is regulated by national legislation and CITES is not relevant. While the parties are required to implement and enforce the Convention, there are no powers, beyond persuasion, to force them to do so. Nevertheless much has been done over the years to bring parties into conformity and, under Resolution Conf. 8.4, the Secretariat has the authority to identify and report upon non-compliant countries. In relation to other legislation, the Convention neither overrides national and international legislation relating to trade in, taking possession or transport of CITES specimens, including customs, public health, and veterinary matters (Article XIV.2), nor does it affect a number of provisions regarding marine species.

In the light of the importance and impact of trade, many international and United Nations conventions and agreements have been drafted and entered into by countries with a view to conserve endangered species. General Agreement on Trade and Tariffs (hereinafter, GATT) specify certain provisions that may be used by the member countries to regulate their imports and exports. Article I enunciate the principle of 'most favoured nation' to all GATT members. Article XIII states that quantitative restrictions must be applied in a non-discriminatory manner. Article XX gives the general exceptions wherein a contracting party might take measures necessary to protect human, animal or plant life or health – Article XX (b) or, for the conservation of exhaustible natural resources – Article XX (g). The WTO Panel in the Shrimp Turtle case upheld US decision to use TED's to reduce the capturing of turtles along with shrimps though it ultimately ruled against US as it was being discriminatory.

The World Heritage Convention is another tool to preserve endangered fauna. This convention read with the preamble recognizes protection of cultural properties and natural resources and the inter relationship between people and nature. Article 2 defines the term 'natural heritage' as including 'areas which constitute the habitat of threatened species of animals and plants of outstanding universal value from the point of view of science or conservation'.

India is also party to the Convention on the Conservation of Migratory Species of Wild Animals (CMS) which speaks of the importance of cooperation and effective management for conservation of migratory species which migrate outside the national jurisdiction of a member State. Article 1 (i) refers to as 'taking, hunting, fishing capturing, harassing, deliberate killing, or attempting to engage in any such conduct'. Art. 3(5) prohibit the taking of migratory species listed in Appendix I subject to certain exceptions'. Article 5 (5) (j) also states that an agreement concluded by a party should implement a measure to manage the taking of migratory species and Art 5(5) (k) states that procedures to suppress illegal taking should be implemented.

International convention for regulation of whaling prescribes the catch limits, protection of whales and imposes restrictions on hunting methods. In coping with the provisions laid out by the whaling commission, all the cetacean species, i.e., whale, dolphins etc. have been included in Schedule I of Wildlife (Protection) Act, 1972. The convention prohibits the killing, taking, hunting of whales subject to certain exceptions.

The most important piece of legislation for regulation of trade in endangered species is CITES whose main object is to promote international cooperation for protection of certain species of flora and fauna against over exploitation as a result of international trade. Appendix I prohibits trade of the listed species altogether. Appendix II allows the trade of species mentioned provided licenses are granted after in depth scientific scrutiny. Appendix III allows trade of the species mentioned after issuance of certificates and permits. Article 1(c) defines trade as, 'export, re-export, import and introduction from the sea'. CITES requires the setup of a scientific and management authority which has the power to issue permits and licenses for trade of endangered species under Appendix II & III and in exceptional circumstances Appendix I.

Despite being the most promising regulation to minimise illegal trade of endangered species, CITES is also subject to a few limitations. CITES is a non-self-executing treaty which cannot be enforced unless the States implements its provisions in their national legislations. The mere ratification of CITES is not enough. Further India rely more on foreign trade regulations for the implementation of CITES. These laws deal with trade in certain species as restricted or prohibited goods, import and export of which require licenses. These legislations are ill adapted to the specific purposes of CITES. It is suggested that with a federal and parliamentary form of Government in a country like India, the Act should contain all the necessary guidelines, the general layout etc. wherein provisions should be made for the Executive to make regulations.

The financial burden is yet another major problem faced by developing countries like India. The fundamental economic dilemma of conservation comes into play where developing countries in need of funds find it difficult in obtaining them, there is inflexibility of funding eligibility, heavy auditing and reporting requirements.

Another important defect in CITES is that the information in records are different and tampered with. The estimates in international trade in endangered species are poorly documented. Actual trade differs and is more in number than what is recorded in these documents. A large number of these species are traded under forged documents and the imports and exports take place in the porous trans-boundary regions where the trade is not detected due to lack of authorities. For a new species to be listed in CITES, it involves a two third majority at the Conference of Parties, which according to critics is an onerous process and against the precautionary principle which is one of the fundamental objectives of CITES. However, there is a certain degree of flexibility as it does not require consensus based decision making as other conventions.

In Australia, the import of live animals into Australia is controlled by the Environment Protection and Biodiversity Conservation Act 1999, and the Bio-security Act 2015. The Environment Protection and Biodiversity Conservation Act 1999 (the EPBC Act) is the Australian Government's central piece of environmental legislation. It provides a legal framework to protect and manage nationally and internationally important flora, fauna, ecological communities and heritage places – defined in the EPBC Act as matters of national environmental significance. These laws apply to anyone who intends to bring a live exotic animal into Australia. In order to be eligible for import into Australia, a species must be listed on the 'List of

Specimens Taken to be Suitable for Live Import'. Plant and animal specimens considered to be suitable for live import into Australia are listed on the Live Import List. There are procedures available for adding certain species on this list. Thus the working of procedure is opposite to the procedures of import of live animals in India, wherein the animal applied for import is checked whether it is in the schedules of the Wildlife Protection Act, enshrined in the appendices of CITES or is an invasive species under Biodiversity Act and if it does not fall under any of these classifications, it may be suitable for import according to the procedures established, whereas in the Australian legislation, the list of specimens taken to be suitable for live import enshrines a group of both native and non-native species, both provided for or not provided for under the CITES appendices, and any deviation from this fixed list makes such species of animal not available for import. The import and possession of exotic animals under this Act work on a permit system, wherein permission is required from the federal environment department depending on where on the 'Live Import List' such specimen falls. Any contravention of the norms import of exotic animals under this Act makes such animal liable for seizure under Division, Subdivision AA and AB of the Act. Section 444A provides for seizure of specimens involved in a contravention of Part 13A. Part 13A provides for a list of threatened species categorized as extinct, extinct in the wild, critically endangered, endangered, vulnerable and conservation dependent. These pertain to only native species similar to the schedules of the Wildlife Protection Act. However, in addition to this, the Act provides for Seizure of things (other than specimens involved in a contravention of Part 13A) under section 445 under Subdivision AB which empowers an authorized officer to seize a thing if he or she has reasonable grounds to suspect that it is evidential material in relation to an offence against an environmental law, in relation to a contravention of an environmental penalty provision or in relation to both. Sub-section 4 of this section defines a 'thing' to include a vehicle, vessel, aircraft, platform, document, organism and specimen. Thus, the inclusion of the word 'specimen' within its ambit allows the seizure of illegally imported pets. As 'environmental law' is provided to mean The Environment Protection and Biodiversity Act 1999, any contravention against the 'Live Import Lists' or permits included thereof brings within the jurisdiction of this Act, offences pertaining to the illegal trade and ownership of exotic pets. These provisions are in addition to other legislation applied to the import and export of wildlife products, including legislation administered by the Department of Immigration and Border Protection, Department of Agriculture and Water Resources and Therapeutic Goods Administration

US entered ratified the CITES convention in 1974. Prior to US entry into CITES, there were a few legislations that governed trade of endangered species. The Lacey Act of 1900 was enacted which provides for the FWS authority to detain and inspect imported goods of wildlife including the baggage, parcel and vehicles. Lacey Act primarily prohibits the import, export, transport, sale etc. in violation of federal or state or foreign laws concerning wildlife. Under the Lacey Act provisions a defendant may be prosecuted for acting with knowledge of the illegal nature of the crime even if the act is not violating the provisions of the statute. The Lacey Act also prescribes penalties and provides for forfeiture of animal and related articles in case of violation. Under the Migratory Bird Treaty Act, 1918 it is unlawful to hunt, take, purchase or ship etc. of almost all North American birds with the exception of upland game birds. Marine Mammals Protection Act, 1972 which protects and prohibits trade of marine mammals like whales, dolphins, sea lions etc. unless specifically exempted. America's best wildlife trade legislation as yet is the Endangered Species Act, 1973. This Act was enacted to reduce the trade in endangered species. Section 3 defines commercial activity as inclusive of trade. 'Endangered species' means 'any species which is in danger of extinction throughout all or a significant portion of its range other than a species of the Class Insecta determined by the Secretary to constitute a pest whose protection under the provisions of this Act would present an overwhelming and overriding risk to man'. The term 'take' has a comprehensive meaning to include harass, harm, pursue, hunt, etc. section 4 give the basis for determination. Section 9 prohibits import, export, take, deliver, sale of the listed species and section 10 provides the exceptions to section 9. Lastly, section 11 provides the penalties. Trade of endangered species is permitted in special circumstances under such terms and conditions as Secretary may prescribe. The trade under exceptions is limited. In a recent judgment given by the International Court of Justice, (Australia v. Japan) the scientific whaling operations by Japan in the southern ocean or Antarctica was held to be unjustified and not undertaken for the purposes of scientific research. The court ruled that Japan should revoke all the permits given under the JARPAII programme in the southern ocean.

India has always supported the principle of sustainable development. Prior to Wildlife (Protection) Act, 1972 there were the Wild Birds and Animal Protection Act, 1912 and Elephants Protection Act, to regulate trade of endangered species. Now there are numerous provisions in our laws for the protection of wildlife and combating illegal trade in India. The fundamental right to a healthy environment is one of the many facets of the fundamental right to life and personal liberty guaranteed to every person under Article 21 of the Constitution of India. Article 245 gives power to the Parliament to make laws for the whole or any part of the territory of India. Under the concurrent List (List III) the Parliament and State Legislature may make laws on protecting of forests and wildlife. Article 48 of the Constitution states 'the State shall endeavour to protect and improve the environment and to safeguard the forests and wild life of the country'. Article 51 A (g) imposes a fundamental duty on the citizens of India to protect the natural environment including wild life and to have compassion to all living beings. Article 253 empowers the Parliament to make any law for implementing any treaty, agreement, or convention with any other country or implement decisions and resolutions made at any international conference. Environment (Protection) Act, 1986 is the 'umbrella' legislation and an enabling law which provides the general framework for all the environmental policies. It gives powers to the Centre to 'take all measures as is necessary and expedient to protect and improve the environment'. Other legislations which restrict hunting and indiscriminate killing of wildlife are dealt in the Import Export Policy of India, Code of Criminal Procedure, Indian Penal Code, and Prevention of Cruelty to Animals Act etc., section 11 of the Prevention of Cruelty to Animals Act prohibits any person, being even owner from harming or treating the animals with cruelty such as chaining, tethering, torturing the animal by inflicting unnecessary pain, administering injurious drug etc. Endangered species that are killed for their husk, skin, and other properties are mercilessly beaten, tortured, and cruelly cut. This is in direct violation of section 11 of PCTA as well as 51 A (g) of the Constitution of India that states that the animals have to be treated with compassion. Wild birds like parakeets and *mynas* are smuggled in socks, tiny boxes or forever trapped in tiny cages, where their wings are cut with a pair of scissors to prevent them from flying. These activities severely violate PCA Act and Article 51 A (g).

Policy Consideration

Clearly, there is an urgent need to intensify law enforcement efforts against wildlife smuggling. An increase in resources, frequency of law enforcement action, strict corruption-reduction programs among law enforcement officials, toughening of laws (and possibly penalties) and the elimination of legal loopholes would each likely have some positive effect in reducing the trade, given the very low baselines in the wildlife regulation and conservation enforcement. However, the extent of the positive effect remains a question, and there are reasons to doubt how ultimately effective law enforcement against wildlife trafficking can ultimately be. Unlike in the case of other illegal economies, the supply areas for wildlife are extremely extensive and shipments are often small even while the overall volume of traffic is immense, making detection of poaching or hunting extraordinarily difficult. Beyond spot detection, it is hard to imagine how law enforcement could be beefed up to succeed on its own in substantially reducing traffic. Consequently, both the incapacitation and deterrent effects of law enforcement will inevitably remain limited even at far greater enforcement levels.

More often than not, law enforcement simply drives black markets, including in wildlife, underground and out of view as well as to new areas with lesser enforcement, but does not necessarily reduce them. As the previous empirical illustrations show, just like with other illegal economies, law enforcement often also contributes to the vertical integration and professionalization of the wildlife smuggling groups. Such organizational changes, in turn, make criminal groups more lethal and give them the capacity to act on a large-scale, neither of which is a positive outcome from conservation and law enforcement perspectives. The fact that less competent and determined hunters and smugglers may be eliminated from the illegal wildlife market does not inevitably imply a reduction in the incidence and intensity of poaching.

Although creating legal economic alternatives does not address the problem of higher-up traders, it can simplify and focus law enforcement as well as enhance the political sustainability of prohibitions on wildlife trade and reduce political conflict. If people face either dire poverty or wildlife hunting, they will frequently choose wildlife hunting. And in such circumstances if the government attempts to enforce a ban on wildlife hunting, political conflict, leading even to violent opposition, may ensue. Existing militant groups can exploit such situations.

Unlike in the case of other illegal economies, such as the drug trade, the problem that the illegal price and profits will remain higher than profits from the substitute legal economy and hence hunters will not be interested in switching may be somewhat less intense. Since wildlife is a finite commodity, as wild stocks decline, so often do profits for low-level poachers. And even in drugs, price-profitability is not always the most important driver. In fact, a critical component of successful alternative livelihoods schemes to counteract poaching was precisely that they were instituted when wildlife was being depleted and economic interest in poaching was declining. Of course, from a conservation perspective, it is probably too late: the marginalized populations are weaned off of illegality, but the wildlife conservation may still have failed because the species were depleted anyway.

The discussion of the effectiveness of various regulatory measures and policy approaches has revealed the extraordinary complexity and difficult trade-offs among various policy approaches. There are no silver bullets in mitigating the illegal trade in wildlife, despite the extreme urgency and intensity of the problem. Critically, the discussion has shown that the work effectiveness of various policies is often highly contingent – the same regulatory design may work well for a particular species in one country, and be ineffective in another country. Bans may work for some species, but fail for others. Licensing trade in the same species of parrots may work in one region, but fail in another. What this means is that local institutional and cultural settings matter a great deal and that local wildlife factors and species specific factors matter are equally significant. Consequently, a policy can only be effective if it is based on extensive local data and is closely tailored to local conditions. Consequently, a paper such as this one can only offer broad policy recommendations as guidelines for designing a regulatory framework to mitigate the illegal trade in wildlife and enhance conservation.

Conclusion

Illicit wildlife trafficking describes any environment-related crime that involves the illegal trade, smuggling, poaching, capture or collection of endangered species, protected wildlife (including animals and plants that are subject to harvest quotas and regulated by permits), derivatives or products thereof. The demand for wildlife products comes from a number of different consumer groups and is, in some cases, heavily influenced by culture. On one side of the spectrum, there is demand that is fuelled by the perceived medicinal value of some products or the social status that is associated with them. On the other side, there is demand that is fuelled by opportunistic buying and often ignorant tourists who purchase souvenirs or pets to take home.

The issue of illicit wildlife trafficking is almost always seen as an environmental issue first and as a transnational crime and justice issue second. In addition, wildlife crime is known to involve significant organized criminal networks that are engaged in a range of criminal activities. They are responsible for the corruption of officials, fraud, money laundering and violence, causing social unrest and undermining the rule of law and confidence in government institutions. Tackling organized crimes such as illicit wildlife trafficking is essential to secure sustainable economic growth in the continent. It is then of paramount importance that national governments – and regional institutions such as my own – do everything they can to tackle illicit wildlife trafficking. Our approach to tackling illicit wildlife trafficking must be of a magnitude that matches its severity. That means attention from the highest levels of government. The new wave of organized wildlife trade crime with heavily armed groups of poachers acting across borders is jeopardizing conservation successes we had in the past and puts in danger whole ecosystems in many countries. It is thus threatening people's livelihoods and has severe socioeconomic effects for the countries affected.

The current global approach to fighting illicit wildlife trafficking is failing, contributing to the instability of society and threatening the existence of some illegally traded species. The governments and international organizations consulted on this issue agree that the current approach is not sufficient. However, opinions on the responsibility of different actors vary: countries that are primarily associated with demand are concerned with enforcement on the supply side, while countries that are primarily associated with supply are concerned with education and enforcement on the demand side. International organizations and government representatives point out that while there are individuals within governments and international organizations who are passionate about halting illicit wildlife trafficking, it is not a priority for governments.

References

Bennett, E. (2002). Is there a link between wild meat and food security, *Conservation Biology*, 16 (3): 590-592.

Brack, D. and Hayman, G. (2002). *International environmental crime: the nature and control of environmental black markets.* London: Royal Institute of International Affairs.

CITES (2012). *Elephant conservation, illegal killing and ivory trade*. Report to 62nd Standing Committee Meeting: SC62 Doc.46.1, Geneva: CITES.

Davis, B. (2005). *Black market: Inside the endangered species trade in Asia.* San Rafael: Earth Aware Editions.

Department of Environmental Affairs, Republic of South Africa (2012). *Minister Edna Molewa addresses National Press Club on the ongoing scourge of rhino poaching.* Retrieved from http://www.environment.gov.za/?q=content/molewa national pressclub rhinopoaching brieing.

Engler, M. and Parry-Jones, R. (2007). *Opportunity or threat: The role of the European Union in the global wildlife trade*. A TRAFFIC Europe Report, Brussels: TRA-FFIC Europe.

IUCN and Accor (2008). *Biodiversity – my hotel in action: A guide to sustainable use of biological resource*. Gland: IUCN.

Lovgren, S. (2008). Wildlife trade booming in Burmese casino town. *National Geographic*, Retrived from http://news.nationalgeographic.com/news/2008/02/080228-wildlife-trade.html.

Michler, I. (2011). Rhino rage. *African Geographic*, March: 42-50.

Neo, H. M. (2009). *Smuggling wildlife: From eggs in a bra to geckos in underwear.* Referencing John Sellar, chief enforcement officer, CITES, AFP.

Nijman, V. (2010). An overview of international wildlife trade from Southeast Asia. *Biodiversity and Conservation*, 19(4):1101-1114.

Robinson, J. and Bennett, E. (2002). Will alleviating poverty solve the bush meat crisis? *Oryx*, 36(4): 332.

The Association of Southeast Asian Nations Wildlife Enforcement Network (ASEAN-WEN) (2009). *Illegal wildlife trade in Southeast Asia factsheet*. Retrived from http://www.asean-wen.org/index. php? option = com docman & task = doc details & gid = 5 & Itemid = 80.

Schoppe, S. (2009). *Status, trade dynamics, and management of the Southeast Asian box turtle in Indonesia*, Kuala Lumpur: TRAFFIC Southeast Asia.

Sheperd, C. (2000). Export of live freshwater turtles and tortoises from northern Sumatra and Riau, Indonesia: A case study. In Peter Paul Van Dijk et al. (Eds.), *Asian turtle trade: Proceedings of a workshop on conservation and trade of freshwater turtles and tortoises in Asia*, Chelonian Research Monographs No.2, Phnom Penh.

Peter Paul Van Dijk et al. (Eds.) (2000). *Asian turtle trade: Proceedings of a workshop on conservation and trade of freshwater turtles and tortoises in Asia*, Chelonian Research Monographs No.2, Phnom Penh.

TRAFFIC-Southeast Asia Indochina (2004). *The trade in marine turtle products in Vietnam*. Retrived from www.traffic.org/species-reports/traffic species reptiles 23. pdf.

Sinha, S. (2010). *Handbook on wildlife law enforcement in India.* New Delhi: TRAFFIC India.

Srivastava, M. (2010). Tracking thc tiger killers. *India Today,* May 28.

2

Trafficking of Ivory and Rhino Horn

Mai Sato, University of Reading, UK
Mike Hough, Birkbeck University of London, UK

Introduction

This paper develops a conceptual framework within which the policies for the regulation of different forms of wildlife trafficking have been evolved. The framework is intended to be adaptable for a range of trafficking activities, but our framework uses the example of trafficking of illicit rhino horn. There are close similarities between the trafficking of rhino horn and of ivory, and some reference is also made to the latter. We have chosen to focus on horn and ivory, because these markets are highly complex, whose social distance from European crimes makes it heuristically rich.

We shall argue that the distinction between instrumental and normative strategies is a crucial one. Politicians instinctively reach for instrumental ones – primarily those involving criminalization and the use of deterrent threat – but opportunity reduction, obstruction and surveillance also figure here. If these are the obvious and more traditional criminal policy response to tackle wildlife crime, we would argue that more attention should be paid to normative policies. Normative approaches – which aim to change behavioural norms and values – have not been properly examined by research. Studies routinely contain concluding recommendations for a multifaceted approach and recognize the importance of raising awareness and education. But the evidence base on normative strategies, and especially those that focus on demand reduction, remains thin. It is unclear what normative approaches are currently being used, who is using them, and whether they secure a positive response from consumers.

Academic Literature – from Conservation to Crime Control

Besides journals which focus specifically on wildlife protection, the bulk of the academic literature on wildlife crime appears in natural science journals[1]. Articles published in criminology journals are still sporadic though they seem to be receiving greater attention in recent years (e.g. Naylor, 2004; Warchol, 2007; Schneider, 2008; Lemieux & Clark, 2009; Wyatt, 2009; Pires & Moreto, 2011; South & Wyatt, 2011; Wyatt, 2011; Cao & Wyatt, 2013; Kalron, 2013).

Almost all review of natural science literature argued for better 'scientific management and monitoring' (Seidensticker, 2010) of wildlife trade (e.g. Wasser et al., 2004; Blundell & Mascia, 2005; Alacs & Georges, 2008; Gerardo & Ferriss, 2008; Gerson et al., 2008; Wasser et al., 2008; Alacs et al., 2010; Barber-Meyer, 2010; Meyers et al., 2010; Percipalle et al., 2011; Rosen & Smith, 2010; Seidensticker, 2010; Fa et al., 2013). The underlying assumption is that while trafficking of wildlife is estimated to be a multi-billion dollar industry with plants and animals being trafficked each year, wildlife records are 'notoriously unreliable' (Blundell & Mascia, 2005) and that 'scientists have yet to describe the scope and scale of the trade.' (Rosen & Smith, 2010: 24). The reviewed articles proposed various ways in which recent scientific developments can contribute to the reduction of wildlife trafficking:

DNA assignment analysis to help determine the product origin where ivory from African elephants is being removed (Wasser et al., 2004; Wasser et al., 2008); a complementary coding system where by customs authorities adopt an existing taxonomic classification system to standardize, organize and capture wildlife trade data (Gerson et al., 2008); increased collaboration with forensic scientists and conservation geneticists to provide a scientific basis for the development of forensic methods (Alacs & Georges, 2008; Alacs et al., 2010); a DNA bar-coding system to monitor endangered species for investigating semi-processed or, morphologically indistinguishable wildlife products (Meyers et al., 2010); and the improved identification of hotpots threatened by bush meat trade (Fa et al., 2013).

There are divergent views in these natural science papers on how the data should be used. Some argue data should be used to develop effective 'conservation' policy (Barber-Meyer, 2010) and various projects to protect wildlife (e.g. Blundell & Mascia, 2005; Gerardo & Ferriss, 2008; Gerson et al., 2008; Barber-Meyer, 2010; Kagande & Musarurwa, 2014). Others believe scientific techniques can be used specifically for 'crime control' policy aimed at prevention, detection, arrest and prosecution. These studies express a general concern about the low levels of law enforcement (Yu-Ming et al., 2000; Alacs & Georges, 2008) and an expectation that better scientific techniques and better quality data should and can be used in tackling wildlife crime (e.g. Yu-Ming et al., 2000; Wasser et al., 2004; Alacs & Georges, 2008; Alacs et al., 2010; Wasser et al., 2008; Barber-Meyer, 2010; Meyers et al., 2010; Percipalle et al., 2011; Fa et al., 2013). Wasser et al. (2008) states, for example – DNA analysis of the project can help inform authorities how crime syndicates are operating and where to concentrate law-enforcement efforts to stop poaching at its source. With a view to identifying the origin of poached products as well, forced countries should take responsibility for the illegal killing of their wildlife by exposing them to CITES and other internationally enforced sanctions. Cutting off supply can also help thwart the long history of ineffective prosecution of illegal wildlife traffickers in consumer countries.

The call for firmer law enforcement that characterizes the natural science papers – as showcased in the above quote – is premised on the assumption that catching and punishing the 'offender' is the solution to wildlife crime.

In the criminological literature, authors acknowledge that wildlife trafficking – often categorized as part of 'green criminology' – receives 'little attention from the criminological community' (Wyatt, 2011). The limited literature tends to focus on the modus operandi. For example, Wyatt's (2009 and 2011) work on the falcon trade in Russia looked at the mechanics of the illegal trade: who is involved, how it is occurring and where it is taking place. South & Wyatt (2011) compared the trafficking of wildlife and drugs, examining the size of markets and the smuggling operations. Warchol (2007) provides a descriptive analysis of the illegal market in terms of species in demand in South Africa and Namibia, and of the profile of poachers and traffickers. Kalron (2013) criticized the current African anti-poaching and anti-trafficking operations as lacking sophistication and determination, giving criminal organisations an easy ride.

These studies share with natural science papers the advocacy of better law enforcement to curb supply. Exploring the linkage between drug and wildlife smuggling operations, South & Wyatt (2011) argue that the illegal wildlife trade has not attracted the same level of law enforcement resources as 'the war on drugs', and argue that 'law enforcement in both of these areas need to cooperate and share intelligence in order to combat both of these smuggling operations'. Kalron (2013) is probably most outspoken about the need for supply-side strategies that crack down on poaching and trafficking. He argues ...conservation today, at least with regard to several species and regions, is an actual war in the military sense of the word…poaching is no longer a conservationist's or wildlife management problem; it is a national security crisis that needs a national security response. As mentioned above, the need to move from traditional anti-poaching operations to more sophisticated counter-guerrilla warfare is crucial (Kalron, 2013).

However, not all criminologists propose that heavier policing and punishment is the only way forward in managing wildlife trafficking. Pires & Moreto (2011) – through the examination of trade in parrots, wildlife skins and over-fishing - propose a combination of situational crime prevention techniques and the promotion of local incentives to deflect people from poaching. Naylor (2004) offers a historical account of the illicit ivory trade and argues that the heart of the problem and the solution lies with demand. The following quote is a sharp contrast to that of Kalron (2013) above and the other studies calling for supply reduction.

Whatever mix of incentives (to conservation) and disincentives (to unregulated trafficking) may be introduced, it must never be forgotten that protecting wildlife from poachers and smugglers is a necessary but not a sufficient condition to ensure the prosperity of other species. The ultimate regulation necessary is not an effort to control the traffic in this or that form of wildlife, but an attempt to ease and, where possible, reverse the pressures which human beings, with their increasing numbers, their rising consumption levels and their destructive technologies, place on the biosphere as a whole (Naylor, 2004).

This article aligns itself with Naylor's (2004) conclusion that demand reduction of wildlife trade needs to be tackled in consumer countries and that more efforts should be made in understanding values and culture in consumer countries relevant to the conservation of wildlife (Turner, 2004; Singh, 2008; Sebele, 2010; Tisdell et al., 2010; Yu, 2010; Pires & Moreto, 2011; Ayling, 2013a; Ayling, 2013b; Phelps et al., 2013; Ferrie et al., 2014). Previous studies have proposed a multifaceted approach and point out the importance of raising awareness and education. The evidence base on normative strategies, and those that focus on demand reduction, however, remains to be properly explored. This article examines what normative approaches are currently being used, who is using them, and whether they secure a positive response from consumers.

Main Framework – Durkheim's Duality of Human Nature

We think it is helpful to go back to one of sociology's founding fathers to find a conceptual framework for framing policies to manage wildlife trafficking. The distinction between instrumental and normative motivation, which is central to our analysis, derives from Durkheim (1915), who proposed a basic duality in human nature: people's individual personalities coexist with a shared and socially constructed morality. He proposed that variations in personalities could account for differences in self-interested behavior, but in accounting for moral behavior one also had to make reference to the conscious collective.

Policies of social control that are built on assumptions about self-interest are distinct from those that take account of the conscious collective. The former consists of instrumental strategies that manipulate the costs and benefits of behavior. In the context of wildlife products, effort is usually focused on deterrent strategies targeting poachers and traffickers rather than consumers. However there are also secondary instrumental strategies, such as situational crime prevention techniques involving surveillance, opportunity reduction, obstruction and target removal. Examples include the tagging of rhino horn and the dehorning of rhinos.

Policies that exploit features of the conscious collective are normative in their approach, mobilizing or extending people's moral commitment to protect wildlife. The target audience of this approach is typically, but not exclusively comprised of consumers. (Local communities in poaching areas are also potential target audiences.) Examples include campaigns launched by NGOs and 'soft power' diplomacy by politicians. Normative demand reduction strategies aim to shrink the market demand for goods through moral persuasion. In reality, some regulatory strategies are neither exclusively normative nor purely instrumental, but a combination of the two. An example of such a hybrid policy can be found in strategies to co-opt local communities into opposition to poaching by both providing a self-interested incentive (for example by sharing the income from tourism) and a normative one. In conservation terms, this may be termed utilitarian ecology as it values nature for the end-use of human needs and the economic value of eco-tourism – whilst achieving conservation (Stoett, 2002).

Before examining each policy, we should say a little about legalization (or decriminalization) of currently illicit wildlife markets. This is an approach which – depending on how it is put into practice – is neither instrumental nor normative. A counsel of despair would be to suggest that the costs of control will inevitably exceed the benefits of conservation, and that the only realistic approach is to decriminalize, deregulate and accept the inevitable extinction of rhino and elephant. We include such an option not as a serious contender for consideration, but only for the sake of completeness of analysis – though some pessimists see this outcome as inevitable (Naylor, 2004; Ayling, 2013a).

There are intermediate positions, however, between unregulated legalization and criminalization. In 2012, a South African conservationist proposed to the International Wildlife Management Congress that the trading of rhino horns should be legalized (Ayling, 2013a). The sale would be strictly regulated by establishing government-owned or government-regulated agencies that would sell legal horns to certified Asian pharmaceutical companies (Ayling, 2013a). In theory, legalization would reduce the demand for illegal horns by flooding the market with legitimate horn. However, legalization could have the perverse effect of stimulating the market, to a point at which demand could not be met simply by licit supplies. There are added problems with the approach. First, 'production costs' would inevitably be lower for poachers than for farmers, so that the incentive to poach and traffic would remain. Secondly, the very process of legalization would undermine any accompanying normative strategies to reduce demand. In other words, legalization as a policy is inconsistent with any attempts to shape the normative climate that surrounds the purchasing of horn.

Instrumental Approaches: Prosecution, Armed Response and Situational Crime Prevention

South Africa reports a worrying increase in rhino poaching. In 2010, 333 were poached, which grew to 448 in 2011, 668 in 2012 and 946 in 2013 – with annual projections exceeding a thousand by the end of 2014 (South African Department of Environmental Affairs)[2]. In recent years, law enforcement authorities in South Africa have responded to the escalating amount of poaching with stricter penalties, more rangers on the grounds, more weaponry, and military patrols (Ayling, 2013a). The South African arrest statistics reflect the increased efforts made with 165 arrests in 2010, and 330 in 2013 (Department of Environmental Affairs, 2013). Similar initiatives are noted elsewhere, including Kenya.

While South Africa may be putting increasing efforts into punishing those involved in wildlife crime, Ayling (2013a; 2013b) is skeptical that deterrence through law enforcement can prevent wildlife trafficking to a significant degree.

The rewards of the crime are in many cases so great, and the execution of the crime so uncomplicated...punishment for environmental crime is anything but certain. Once common criticism relating to the treatment of TEC (Transnational Environmental Crime) is that it has been 'woefully neglected' by states, with penalties set at far too low a level and enforcement against offenders often lax (Ayling, 2013b).

Even where tough laws do exist, it is difficult to prove beyond all reasonable doubt that a poacher is guilty. To ensure a successful prosecution, it often requires DNA analysis linking the rhino carcass, the horn and the poacher, but the expertise is often not available for this type of sophisticated analysis (Adams, 2012). States are increasingly using scientific techniques to detect and prosecute, as well as using situational crime prevention techniques to make it impossible or more difficult to poach. These include dehorning, poisoning horns, GPS tracking of rhinos, and DNA bar-coding (e.g. Alacs & Georges, 2008; Alacs et al., 2010; Barber-Meyer, 2010; Meyers et al., 2010; Ayling, 2013a; Fa et al., 2013).

Law enforcement officers, however, are not the only ones relying on high-end equipment and scientific techniques. Poachers range from poor villagers to organized crime syndicates who take horns themselves or provide incentives for villagers to do so (Pires & Moreto, 2011; Ayling, 2013a; Kalron, 2013). Therefore, some poachers have access to advanced technologies to kill or disable the animals, including helicopters, night vision goggles, tranquilizing drugs, high-powered weapons and silencers (Ayling, 2013a). Furthermore, poaching and trafficking strategies are constantly renewed and are often sophisticated enough to penetrate the agencies tasked with stopping them (Kalron, 2013; Kagande & Musarurwa, 2014). This makes instrumental approaches costly – if deployed with sufficient intensity to have any real effect.

In addition, controlling the trafficking of wildlife is complicated by its multijurisdictional nature. It is difficult to establish and manage effective cross-border collaboration (Ayling, 2013b), and disparity in sentencing policies between countries makes it even more difficult for all countries involved to make wildlife trafficking a priority. For example, in Zambia, offenders convicted of possession or poaching of rhino horn can receive a sentence of 20 years. In Kenya, the penalty for poaching was until recently simply a fine (Adams, 2012). Recent Kenyan legislation now provides for lengthy prison sentences, however.

Corruption also adds to the difficulty of pursuing the offenders at the top of the trafficking chains that instrumental policies attempt to target. Warchol (2004) found through interviews conducted with US embassy officials in South Africa and Namibia that corruption is endemic among low-paid law enforcement officers, and that embassy staff from Asia and the Middle East are also involved in the illegal trade. He also notes that corruption is not limited to officials but widespread among managers of game reserves, employees of safari hunt companies and rangers in national parks (Warchol 2004; Ayling 2013b). Prosecution – if it happens – tends to be focused on the most marginalized groups involved in low-level activity rather than those involved at a higher level.

The most extreme form of instrumental policy used in controlling horn and ivory poaching is armed response, sometimes referred to as 'shoot to kill'. This strategy is adopted by many national parks game reserves such as in Zimbabwe, South Africa, Kenya and India, and allows police or civilian rangers to shoot the poachers – also often heavily armed – as a last resort inself-defence[3]. The legal protection afforded to rangers who shoot poachers varies from jurisdiction to jurisdiction; sometimes the rangers have the status of police reservists. It is reported that 'shoot to kill' in some jurisdictions is not only tolerated but sometimes encouraged (and rewarded where bravery is shown), to maximize deterrent impact[4]. In Kaziranga for example, the forest guards have immunity from prosecution for shooting a poacher, whether in self-defence or as a proactive ambush or attack (Warchol, 2007).

Armed response strategies of this sort raise difficult ethical issues. Whether protocols are in place – and are actually used – to regulate rangers' use of lethal force will vary from jurisdiction to jurisdiction. Whether the basic intention of the armed response is to secure arrests or actually to shoot the poachers is arguably immaterial in situations where armed resistance is encountered. Perhaps the key ethical – and legal – issue is whether reasonable efforts are made to secure arrests, prior to the use of firearms.

As jurisdictions improve their detective and prosecutorial capacity, and as court sentences are toughened up, it remains to be seen whether these instrumental strategies achieve any real purchase on the problem. On the one hand, the available penalties facing poachers are becoming much more severe – and if they resist arrest they run a significant risk of being shot. On the other hand, there has been little or no read-across to wildlife trafficking from the lessons about supply reduction strategies in drug trafficking. MacCoun and Reuter (2001) have argued that supply-side strategies to contain drug smuggling can have a range of perverse effects. A basic economic principle is that markets translate risk into price. If law enforcement strategies increase the risks of detection and punishment, in markets where demand is buoyant this will simply increase the cost of the product – and make the market more lucrative for those who are prepared to remain in business. And it is important to ask who is most likely to remain within increasingly risky markets: risk drives out the risk-averse, making illicit drug markets increasingly violent. Finally, in drug trafficking at least, the process of removing key participants from the trafficking process creates 'employment opportunities' or 'promotion opportunities' for others. For these reasons, drug trafficking systems have proved highly resilient in the face of enforcement. At present, it is unclear whether similar considerations apply to the trafficking of horn and ivory.

A less aggressive form of instrumental strategy is to focus on prevention rather than dealing with the crime post-hoc through the criminal justice system. A situational crime prevention technique such as dehorning, which renders rhinos worthless to poachers – at least until their horns grow back – may seem like a promising policy. While dehorning is reported to have contributed to the protection of rhinos in Namibia in the 1990s and more recently across other African nations, there are downsides to this practice[5]. Dehorning is costly and needs to be repeated two or more times over the life of a rhino. There is also security cost involved in protecting horns against theft, following dehorning[6]. It is also an intrusive procedure, with risks to the rhino during operations. A further critique – which is levelled at most situational crime prevention techniques – is that dehorning does nothing to address the root causes of poaching such as economic deprivation and societal inequality that exist in these countries (Von Lampe, 2011; Ayling, 2013b). The weight that should be attached to this critique depends on the extent to which blocked opportunities for poaching of rhinos lead to displacement to other forms of poaching, or indeed, other forms of crime. The evidence about displacement – drawn from other forms of offending – is that opportunity reduction rarely results in 100% displacement.

Normative Approaches: Soft Law, Soft Power Diplomacy and Campaigns

As noted above, normative approaches involve reshaping shared norms and values – or to use Durkheimian language, it is about extending the conscious collective. In the case of trafficking of horn and ivory, normative strategies have focused largely on demand reduction, and three main approaches have been followed: the development of international law; the use of 'soft power diplomacy'; and publicity campaigns.

In approaches relying on international law and soft power diplomacy, the aim is to stimulate state-level intervention which in turn – it is hoped – will have an impact on the publicly shared norms and values of citizens in those states. Publicity campaigns, by contrast, aim to achieve a direct impact on citizens' norms and values.

The reader may wonder why we have treated the development of international law (and soft power diplomacy) as normative rather than instrumental strategies. This is because – at least in the field of wildlife trafficking – there are no significant mechanisms to permit the enforcement of the resultant international laws. Even if they appear on the surface to involve the development of instrumental levers, in reality their intended function is to achieve a normative shift within governments (i.e. at state level), which then cascades down to the broader population. To use Durkheimian language, the aim is to extend the conscious collective to other states whereas publicity campaigns directly target individuals throughout the population.

The term 'norm diffusion' in international relations literature is often used to describe the function performed by international organisations including NGOs as they spread the relevant norms to politicians and officials at state level (Finemore, 1996). One can differentiate between horizontal norm diffusion, where one state deploys diplomacy to persuade another state that a particular behavior is wrong, and vertical norm diffusion, where national or international bodies aim to achieve normative shifts in the general population (or relevant sub-groups).

International Organizations and CITES

The Convention on International Trade in Endangered Species of Wild Fauna and Flora (CITES) is the leading international legal framework for regulating the international trade in wildlife. CITES had a membership reaching 180 countries in 2013[7]. Species protected by CITES are listed in three appendices attached to the convention, with Appendix I being the most restrictive. Appendix I lists species threatened with extinction: commercial trade is prohibited, and trade in specimens of these species is permitted only in exceptional circumstances such as trophy hunting[8].

By becoming a party to CITES, a state chooses to become a member and pledges to adopt rules to monitor, regulate or ban international trade in species under threat. While CITES is legally binding on signatory states, who are thus expected to implement the convention in their domestic legislation, the initiative to become a signatory necessarily has to come from the relevant state. Similar to other soft laws, CITES is also presented as 'a framework to be respected by each Party' to implement appropriate domestic laws and monitor trade. In other words, norm diffusion occurs when a state joins CITES, thereby making a normative commitment to the international community to protecting wildlife. It thus serves both declaratory and symbolic functions to the international community. However, whether CITES is effective in regulating wildlife trade is another matter, as illegal trading in wildlife has continued throughout the forty year lifespan of the convention (Ayling, 2013b). Lemieux and Clarke (2009) examined the effectiveness of the CITES ban on the African ivory trade. They report that the continent's overall elephant population increased after the elephant was moved from Appendix II to I, but that in some African countries substantial and growing numbers of elephants continued to be poached. They found that variation in the effects of the ban is partly explained by the regulations in place for domestic trade. Countries with an unregulated domestic market allowed poaching to continue, and ivory purchased in these countries by wholesalers was trafficked throughout Africa and Asia.

The efforts by signatory states to translate responsibilities under CITES into domestic legislation also seem to impact the effectiveness of the rhino horn ban. During the 1970s and 1980s the 85 per cent fall in the rhino population led to them being listed in Appendix I of CITES, which instituted a ban on international trade in rhino horns (Ayling, 2013b)[9]. Rhino horns between the late 1970 and 1990s were in high demand for medicine in Asia and for jambiya dagger handles in Yemen (Ellis, 2013). Success stories in banning rhino horn trade through accession to CITES – and more specifically the signatory states' commitment to enforcing the ban through domestic legislation following membership – can be found in Japan, South Korea, and Yemen (Ellis, 2013). Vietnam and China – despite both countries being member states of CITES – have yet to reduce the trade in illegal rhino horns through domestic legislation.

For example, in the 1970s, Japan was the primary consumer of rhino horn in Asia for medicinal purposes. Japan ratified CITES in 1980 and upon joining, the Ministry of Health required all manufacturers of rhino horn medicines to find substitutes for their products (Ellis, 2013)[10]. In Yemen, thorough domestic legislation and the expansion of staff involved in wildlife conservation at the upgraded Environment Protection Agency also eradicated the demand for rhino horn (Ellis, 2013). By contrast, in China and Vietnam, even though both countries are members of CITES as of 1981 and 1994 respectively, there was lacks of political will to follow through the responsibilities in CITES. What the above examples shows is that ratification of 'CITES is not an end in itself, but a tool to be used to assist real conservation actions' (Arroyo-Quiroz et al., 2005).

A separate issue to the enforcement of CITES is the politics behind the decisions by states to become signatories to the convention. From its original membership of 20 states in 1975 to the 2013 membership of 180 states, members have notionally joined voluntarily, and have had the freedom to withdraw any time. The growth in membership appears to reflect an expansion of the conscious collective in the international community in relation to wildlife protection. This analysis, however, misses the important point that some signatories to CITES are effectively coerced into membership. Arroyo-Quiroz et al. (2005) explains that Mexico 'ratified CITES only as a result of external and internal pressure' from the US but it did not actively participate in the discussion of CITES nor implement any effective domestic legislation. It was only years later that Mexico finally recognized environmental concerns and national legislation was enacted in 2000 (Arroyo-Quiroz et al., 2005)[11]. Singh (2008) also provides a history of how Laos was pressured into entering CITES. He argued that:

Popular representations of wildlife trade promoted by conservation organizations construct an image of regulation through CITES as a global necessity. The assumed morality of such interventions can provoke counter accusations about the immorality of impositions by Western conservationists (Singh, 2008).

A further point regarding CITES is that active member states committed to conservation may 'project an appearance of unified potency' but are in reality 'divided and weak' (Singh, 2008). The conscious collective that CITES represents in protecting wildlife is made up of state parties that believe in different approaches to conservation: the Southern African countries want a policy for sustainable use of wildlife whereas parties in developed countries and in East Africa take a protectionist stand to the preservation of wildlife (Arroyo-Quiroz et al., 2005).

Soft Power Diplomacy

Soft power diplomacy is a concept developed by Joseph Nye in his book Soft Power – The Means to Success in World Politics. Nye (2004) argues that post-September 11, soft power diplomacy is increasingly being used as opposed to the more familiar hard power diplomacy which rests on inducements or threats. He defines soft power as 'getting others to want to do the outcome that you want' and that it 'rests on the ability to shape preferences of others' (Nye, 2004). He draws analogies to relationships and marriages stating that power between two people is not decided by size or strength but in the 'mysterious chemistry of attraction' (Nye, 2004). In politics, Nye (2004) describes this process as follows:

A country may obtain the outcomes it wants in world politics because other countries – admiring its values, emulating its example, aspiring to its level of prosperity and openness – want to follow it.

Hard and soft power diplomacies are not complete opposites but a spectrum of behaviors designed to achieve outcomes. At one end of the scale is command power and on the other end is co-optive power (Nye, 2004). In between exists coercion, inducement, agenda setting, and attraction, where the former being hard and the latter being soft power. Hard power uses resources such as force, sanction, payments and bribes whereas soft power uses institutions, values, culture and policies (Nye, 2004). According to the annual Monocle soft power survey, the UK was ranked second in the world in the 2013 survey. The country's soft power is reported to rest on the friendly relationships it has with the Commonwealth nations and the prominence and the high respect held for the BBC, among other factors.

The UK has also been making use of its soft power on wildlife protection[12]. The UK government in February 2014 hosted an international conference on illegal wildlife trade, which brought together global leaders around the world with the aim to 'agree a high level political commitment to take urgent action to tackle illegal wildlife trade'[13]. Among the participants were icons of the 'UK brand' – including two members of the royal family. Using soft power, the conference was an attempt to send a normative message about the commitment of the UK towards tackling illegal wildlife and 'softly' urging other countries to follow.

What soft power diplomacy aims to do is to extend the conscious collective of one or more states to other states. In other words, as discussed above, soft power diplomacy has a horizontal structure, with the norm diffuser and its target being at the same organizational level. This can be contrasted with the work of international organisations where there is typically a vertical relationship between the norm diffuser and its targets in the general population. Whilst the state-to-state directness of soft power diplomacy can be strengthen, problems can emerge when there are tensions between the various agendas that a country is pursuing through soft power diplomacy.

China for example has since 2000 made commitments to African countries to provide soft loans in the arenas of health, humanitarian assistance, and cultural exchanges (Cook, 2009). The primary consideration is economic development and economic partnership, which does not sit comfortably with wildlife conservation agendas. Thus in Kenya, China recently signed an agreement to rebuild the railway line from Mombasa to Nairobi, with plans to extend this to Uganda, Rwanda, Burundi and South Sudan[14]. This would help Kenya's mining and other industries, but some conservationists are concerned that this is going to provide easier access for ivory poachers and middlemen as the railway line runs through Tsavo National Park[15].China is currently the main destination country for illegally trafficked ivory[16].

For some countries, China may not fit Nye's (2004) definition of an attractive model country whose values and culture they wish to adopt. However Cook (2009) has observed that for many African countries, China's economic strength is a source of soft power. China's economic engagement is seen as pragmatic as and more in line with African priorities than western engagement, which often includes humanitarian programs on human rights which are sometimes seen as condescending and hypocritical. There are thus two competing forces on the stage of soft power diplomacy: those countries whose appeal lies in promoting the protection of Africa's wildlife and those like China whose appeal is to be found in its economic strength – and which, some might argue, benefits from the illegal wildlife trade.

Campaign

In the last few years, high profile figures – such as President Barack Obama, Ban Ki-moon, Leonardo DiCaprio, and Jackie Chan – have taken an interest in endangered wildlife and have made public statements in an attempt to raise public awareness of the issue[17]. Academics such as Wyatt (2011) and Ayling (2013a) also support demand reduction approaches, through awareness raising and education, as part of the solution to wildlife trafficking. While campaigns aimed at changing attitudes of consumers are starting to grow, there has been little discussion about the rationale behind these campaigns in the light of what is known about norm transmission.

Campaigns, as noted above, are often launched by international organisations or NGOs. In the context of trafficking of rhino horns, the campaigns are targeted on Asian countries, with Vietnam (and to some extent China) being the main consumer of rhino horns. Rhino horns are popular along the Vietnamese 'new rich' (Ellis, 2013). Rhino horn symbolizes status amongst the wealthy elite, and is used in business deals and social gatherings, where it is ground to a powder, mixed with water and drunk as a social drink (Ellis, 2013; Ayling, 2013a). It is also being sought as a cure for cancer used in tandem with chemotherapy, as the rhino horn is believed to minimize the harmful effects of the other treatments.

There is no scientific evidence for any medicinal value of rhino horn, which is composed of keratin, just like human hair and fingernails (Ayling, 2013a)[18].

Against this background, there are broadly two types of campaigns aimed at tackling demand. One approach (Example 1) is to highlight the cruelty of rhino horn poaching and emphasizes how close rhinos are to extinction. Jackie Chan in a WildAid[19] campaign video calls for the protection of the 'beautiful creature' from poaching while demonstrating the cruelty of poaching through his martial arts skills. The other approach is to challenge the false beliefs that can underpin consumer demand, exemplified by traditional Chinese medicine's assumptions about the curative properties of rhino horns.

Example 1

Jackie Chan: https://www.youtube.com/watch?v=yccID-2jlfM

Example 2

Horns as finger nails: http://wwf.panda.org/?208289/Ad-campaign-aims-to-reduce-Vietnamese-demand-for-rhino-horn

What do these campaigns tells us about the current approaches to norm diffusion? Acharya (2004) states that constructivist scholarship on norms tends to focus on moral transformation whereby 'good' global norms – in this case care for endangered species – prevail over 'bad' local beliefs and practices; but he argues that 'many local beliefs are themselves part of a legitimate order which conditions the acceptance of foreign norms.' This perspective which takes a step back from focusing on how to change people's views and rather looks at whose views the campaigns are trying to impact. Campaigns carry the inherent risk of audience resistance, as there is always a danger that the target audience may construe the message as an unjustified imposition on their own standards.

Hirata (2005) uses the example of Japan's persistent support for whaling, explaining that the Japanese public perceives anti-whaling campaigns as a reflection of cultural imperialism. To the Japanese, it is hypocritical that Westerners consider it morally wrong to kill some mammals such as whales but acceptable to kill others such as sheep or pigs. Most Japanese continue to believe that Japan as a whole has had a distinctive whale-eating culture, regarding whales as fish rather than mammals and thus not deserving of special treatment, and that Japanese have the right to hunt and eat whale as long as stocks are maintained at a sustainable level (Hirata, 2005). Naylor (2004), referring to the ivory campaign, also argues that the photos of decapitated elephants produced a sense of revulsion against ivory in the west but had no real effect in the east where ivory has a long association with art and culture, and the 'thrill of possessing a forbidden object'.

Wildlife campaigns premised on the intrinsic value of protecting rhinos may end up simply preaching to the converted. Campaigns that fail to address cultural values within target audiences seem likely to fail. For example, Yu (2010) argues that Confucian philosophy which dominates in China construes wildlife as a lower life form that can be contained and consumed, and treated as a resource in a utilitarian way. Furthermore, attempts to correct misconceptions as in the poster about keratin described above, may seem to Western sensibilities both witty and logical; but they fail to engage with the belief in traditional oriental medicine that the spirit of the animal is embodied in its flesh and bones; to those who hold these beliefs, the absence of scientific proof of medicinal qualities is irrelevant.

Durkheim in explaining the notion of the conscious collective stated that 'we must not say that an action shocks the conscious collective because it is criminal, but rather it is criminal because it shocks the conscious collective' (Durkheim, 1893 in Giddens, 1972). This brings us to questions about the factors that can shape and expand the conscious collective? Acharya (2004) argues norm diffusion requires 'norm localization' where 'local agents reconstruct foreign norms to ensure the norm fits with the agents' cognitive priors and identities'[20]. He argues that norm localization may be a precondition for the adoption of external norms, and that this process of localization needs to demonstrate that the norms in question have 'a potential to contribute to the legitimacy and efficacy of existing institutions without undermining them significantly'. He also argues that there must be 'willing and credible local actors….these actors should not be seen as 'stooges' of outside forces' (Acharya, 2004).

Applying the above framework, it is not a surprise that the Japanese whaling campaigns to date have been unsuccessful. Greenpeace Japan adopted the anti-whaling campaign used by International Greenpeace headquarters and this did not fit well with the domestic value system, and was not able to create a social movement (Hirata, 2005). Other Japanese NGOs did not join in the movement because they feared that involvement in the anti-whaling cause would damage their reputation, alienate them from the public, and weaken their efforts to raise funds and increase membership (Hirata, 2005). Jackie Chan, as in the example above, in this sense may be a suitable candidate for delivering a message to the 'Asian' market. However, his campaign is heavily endorsed by non-Asian international organizations and NGOs, whose logos are prominent on the campaign materials. It would be interesting to find out how the campaign is received locally. Lastly, Yu (2010) proposes that instead of Confucian philosophy, Daoist philosophy may be useful in the localization process. Daoist philosophy is non-hierarchical in its conceptualization of differences between species, its inclusive and holistic view of all forms of existence calls for harmony among man, nature, and wildlife (Yu, 2010).

Hybrid Policies: Incentivizing Local Communities and Community-based Conservation

In practice, some strategies for regulating undesirable behavior include both instrumental and normative elements. There are two ways in which this may happen. First, normative pressures may be applied at one level – for example by one government upon another, using soft power diplomacy – and these may result in the latter passing and enforcing tough legislation. In other words, the strategy of the government exercising soft power operates both at a normative and at an instrumental level, with the normative levers being applied at the political level, resulting in state deployment of instrumental strategies.

The second way in which instrumental and normative strategies may be combined is when levers applied to a given group have both normative and instrumental dimensions. The clearest example in the case of wild life trafficking is in strategies targeting the communities within which poaching takes place. Twenty or so years ago, poachers would be drawn mainly from local communities living on or near game reserves. The aim of poaching (or hunting) was to protect crops or to market horn or ivory (Warchol, 2007). Back then, the level of organization of poachers was described as 'non-existent to, at best, a loosely associated network of friends or fellow collectors' (Warchol, 2007). Participants would almost certainly have resisted the label of 'poacher', and might well have been proud of their economically valuable skills.

Today, the profile of poachers is polarized between locals and organized crime syndicates (Kalron, 2013). While poor villagers from rural areas are still engaged in poaching, there is growing evidence that organized criminal groups such as Groenewald gang and the ChumlongLemtongthai group are involved (Ayling, 2013a; Killing for Profit, n.d[21]). Often however, organized crime groups are unable to operate without the support of people from local communities.

Promising hybrid policies include those that target local communities in wildlife areas, simultaneously offering tangible benefits from involvement in conservation and promoting the ethical arguments for conservation. This is often referred to as community-based conservation (CBC), operating under the slogan 'protection by, for and with the local communities' (Save the Rhinos, n.d[22]). CBC projects include eco-tourism, production and selling of local craft-work, hunting and collecting traditional medicine products, and running environmental educational programs. The goal is 'to integrate the communities into the projects for profitable cohabitation for all' (Save the Rhinos, n.d).

CBC emerged against a history of exclusion of local communities from the conservation agenda (Turner, 2004; Sebele, 2010). Before CBC, the conservation model was based on 'a romantic European understanding of nature as fragile and pristine' (Turner, 2004) in which human activity was viewed as intrinsically harmful to nature. This led to the creation of protected areas from which local people were excluded. The concept of community engagement started to emerge in developing countries in the 1950s and 60s when developing countries were being decolonized (Selebe, 2010) – an added impetus being the practical impossibility of excluding communities from protected areas through fences, fines, and coercion (Turner, 2004). It was considered that the route to sustainable development was to remove the stigma of charity by involving local people in decision making (Selebe, 2004).

Sebele (2010) evaluated the Khama Rhino Sanctuary Trust; a CBC in Botswana established in 1992 and aimed at saving rhinos and bringing economic benefits for locals through tourism. She shows that the Sanctuary offered employment for the locals such as through the hiring of cleaners, drivers, and guides, but argued that insufficient profit had been generated to permit reinvestment in projects benefitting the community at large. Turner (2004) in examining the CBC of Kruger National Park in South Africa, argues that while tourism has substantial promise, relying on conservation-based tourism for development is a risky business because many community-based projects are not well positioned to compete against state-supported protected areas or private ventures[23].This is because the communities mostly targeted for CBC projects tend to be those which have been disadvantaged by prior conservation initiatives and by colonial legacies which make it more difficult for community actors to engage with their partners on an equal basis (Turner, 2004).

Selebe (2010) also identifies the more critical problem that it is very hard, in practice, to generate a sense of broad-based community ownership of projects. Focus group research with community members in the Sanctuary project showed that they saw control as vested in a single elite family, with heavy reliance on foreign donors (Sebele, 2010). Sebele found that local people were not involved in decision making, and did not directly benefit from the venture. Turner (2004) also identifies the lack of substantial community involvement. He argues that while CBC can take various forms, the majority of projects have a top-down approach, which starts with the government or private actors deciding to involve the local communities near the protected areas, and offering brief consultations with local communities rather than substantial involvement in decision making.

While Sebele (2010) remains hopeful that with more interaction between the locals and those who manage the Sanctuary, CBC can provide for the conservation of natural resources and increase local benefits, Turner (2004) provides a critique of the rationale for CBC from a historical perspective. He argues that CBC projects have focused too much on the material benefit that it promises to bring (although evidence that this occurs is patchy) and have largely ignored the history of many African nations, and questions whether financial benefit is what the local community really want:

CBNRM[24] emerged from a conservation history deeply intertwined with injustice, exclusion and dislocation, and it is far from clear that a largely materialist strategy can respond adequately to this legacy. Although the Makuleke people hope that the conservation future of the Makuleke Region will improve their economic condition, for example, it's not the only basis on which they judge succcss. They see regaining title to their ancestral home as an immense symbolic achievement, the value of which is largely independent of subsequent commercial success or failure....Ultimately, these factors, rather than the material benefits flowing from economic development may prove to be the determinants of CBNRM 'success' (Turner, 2004).

Those who are implementing conservation programs may see poachers as motivated by need (to prevent wild animals from disrupting their farming) or greed (to profit from the sale of wildlife), and may see incentivizing communities to engage in conservation through their integration into the tourism trade as the win-win solution. The caution here is that we need to make sure – through communication with the communities - that the incentives that are offered are consistent with their basic values and outlook.

Conclusion

This paper has reviewed a range of approaches to the reduction of wildlife poaching and trafficking, focusing – but not exclusively – on the poaching of rhinos and the trafficking of rhino horn. We have argued that instrumental strategies to do with arrest, prosecution and punishment of those involved in poaching and trafficking will never be more than one part of the solution to the problem. We suggest that normative strategies are needed to support instrumental strategies. These need to target both the consumers of wild-life products – with the intention of reducing demand – and those who are involved in parts of the supply process.

To be effective, demand-reduction strategies will probably involve soft power diplomacy to secure the support of politicians in consumer countries, coupled with campaigns that direct reach consumers directly. It seems likely that soft power diplomacy will need to encourage new signatories to CITES to take their obligations seriously, and to enact local legislation. It is hard to see how supply reduction strategies will work effectively without well thought-through strategies involving deterrence and situational crime prevention. However, these also need to be combined with strategies that include a normative dimension. The clearest example of this is to be found in community-based conservation programmes that offer local communities both an economic and an ethical stake in the protection of wildlife.

Notes

1. *IngentaConnect* was used to review literature on wildlife trafficking in natural and social sciences.
2. See Department of Environmental Affairs in South Africa: https://www.environment.gov.za/mediarelease/update on rhino poaching.
3. Save the Rhino, 'Shoot to Kill?' : http://www.savetherhino.org/rhino_info/thorny issues/shoot to kill.
4. In Kaziranga National Park, India, forest guards receive a cash bonus to their salary if they successfully wound and kill a poacher.
5. See Save the Rhinos, 'Dehorning' from: http://www.savetherhino.org/rhino_info/issues for debate/de-horning.
6. The actual cost depends on several factors, but current published estimates for dehorning range from US $620 (Kruger National Park) per animal to US$1,000 (private land). It is estimated that it would cost around US$5.8-8.8 million for a one-off dehorning of all the rhinos in Kruger National Park (Save the Rhinos website).
7. CITES (2013),What is CITES? See: http://www.cites.org/eng/disc/what.php
8. Appendix II includes species not necessarily threatened with extinction, but in which trade must be controlled in order to avoid utilization incompatible with their survival.
9. The Southern White rhino was moved to Appendix II in 1994 for the South African population and 2004 for the Swaziland population (Ayling 2013a).

10. The use of manufactured medicines in Japan meant the use of rhino horn was easier to control, as the products were mostly registered with the government in the country of manufacture and one company dominated the manufacture of rhino horn. (Ellis 2013).
11. Arroyo-Quiroz et al. (2005) also makes a point that the implementation and enforcement of CITES represents a significant challenge and is not something that can be done quickly especially for a developing country like Mexico.
12. The UK ranked first in the 2012 survey. For 2013 results, see Monocle Soft Power Survey 2013:http://monocle.com/film/Affairs/soft-power-survey-2013/.
13. London Illegal Wildlife Conference website: https://www.gov.uk/government/topical-events/illegal-wildlife-trade-2014/about.
14. BBC News, 12 May 2014, 'China to build new East Africa railway line' http://www.bbc.com/news/world-africa-27368877.
15. African Wildlife Conservation and Kenya's Wildlife Policy Act, See: http://blogs.cfr.org/campbell/2014/06/11/african-wildlife-conservation-and-kenyas-wildlife-policy-act/.
16. BBC News, 12 April 2012, The illegal ivory trade threatening Africa's elephants. http://www.bbc.co.uk/news/world-17675816.
17. See for example: 'Ban Ki-moon to warn UN Security Council of dangers of wildlife trafficking', The Guardian (28 May 2013). http://www.theguardian.com/world/2013/may/28/un-ban-kimoon-wildlife-trafficking-central-africa Jackie Chan: Chinese attitudes to illegal wildlife products are changing: http://www.theguardian.com/environment/2014/feb/13/jackie-chan-chinese-attitudes-illegal-wildlife-products-change.
18. Most traditional Chinese medicine countries in Asia, including China, Japan, Taiwan, and South Korea, but excluding Vietnam, have removed rhino horn from their traditional medicine pharmacopoeias (Ayling 2013a).
19. Wild Aid is an NGO with a mission to end the illegal wildlife trade by reducing demand through public awareness campaigns and providing comprehensive marine protection. WildAid focuses on reducing the demand for these products, with the strong and simple message: *when the buying stops, the killing can too. See: http://wildaid.org/media.*
20. Achrya (2004) uses the example of ASEAN's response to security norms of the post-Cold War era in explaining the norm localization process.
21. Killing for Profit website: http://killingforprofit.com
22. Save the Rhinos. See: http://www.savetherhino.org/our work/what we do/community conservation.
23. He adds that even though the ethos of CBC is to provide equal opportunities for locals, tourism in southern Africa to be radicalized where white guides are assisted by unskilled black labourers (Turner 2004).
24. CBNRM stands for Community-Based Natural Resource Management.

References

Acharya, A. (2004). How ideas spread: where norms matter? Norm localization and institutional change. *International Organization*, 58(2): 239-275.

Adams, L. (2012). *Shoot to kill?* Save the Rhinos, Retrived from http://www. savetherhino. org/rhino info/thorny issues/shoot to kill.

Alacs, E. & Georges, A. (2008). Wildlife across our borders: A review of the illegal trade in Australia. *Australian Journal of Forensic Sciences*, 40(2): 147-160.

Alacs, E.A., Georges, A., FitzSimmons, N.N. & Robertson, J. (2010). DNA detective: a review of molecular approaches to wildlife forensics. *Forensic Science, Medicine, and Pathology*, 6: 180-194.

Ayling, J. (2013a). What sustains wildlife crime? Rhino horn trading and the resilience of criminal networks. *Journal of International Wildlife Law & Policy*, 16(1): 57-80.

Ayling, J. (2013b). Harnessing third parties for transnational environmental crime prevention. *Transnational Environmental Law*, 2: 339-362.

Arroyo-Quiroz, I., Perez-Gil, R. & Leader-Williams, N. (2005). Developing countries and the implementation of CITES: The Mexican experience. *Journal of International Wildlife Law & Policy*, 8(1): 13-49.

Barber-Meyer, S.M. (2010). Dealing with the clandestine nature of wildlife-trade market surveys. *Conservation Biology*, 24(4): 918-923.

Blundell, A.G. & Mascia, M.B. (2005). Discrepancies in reported levels of international wildlife trade. *Conservation Biology*, 19: 2020-2025.

Cao, A. & Wyatt, T. (2013). A green criminological exploration of illegal wildlife trade in Vietnam. *Asian Criminology*, 8: 129-142.

Cook, J.G. (2009). China's soft power in Africa. In McGiffert, C. (Eds.), *Chinese soft power and its implications for the United States: Competition and cooperation in the developing world.* Centre for Strategic & International Studies. Washington, DC.

Durkheim, E. (1915). *The elementary forms of the religious life*. Retrived from http:/ /www.gutenberg.org/files/41360/41360-h/41360-h.htm.

Durkheim, E. (1893). The division of labour in society. In Giddens, A. (1972), *Emile Durkheim Selected Writings*. Cambridge: Cambridge University Press.

Ellis, K. (2013). *Tackling the demand for rhino horn.* Save the Rhinos, Retrived from http://www. savetherhino.org/rhino info/thorny issues/tackling the demand for rhino horn.

Fa, J.E. et al. (2013). Mapping hotspots of threatened species traded in bushmeat markets in the cross-Sanaga rivers region. *Conservation Biology*, 28(1): 224-233.

Gerson, H. et al. (2008). Monitoring international wildlife trade with coded species data. *Conservation Biology*, 22(1): 4-7.

Hirata, K. (2005). Why Japan support whaling. *Journal of International Wildlife Law & Policy*, 8(2-3): 129-149.

Kalron, N. (2013). Neo-conservation. *African Security Review*, 22(3): 160-166.

Kagande, S.M. & Musarurwa, L.K. (2014). Conserving the African rhinoceros. *Biodiversity and Conservation*, 23: 497-502.

Lemieux, A.D. & Clarke, R.V. (2009). The international ban on ivory sales and its effects on the elephant poaching in Africa. *British Journal of Criminology*, 49: 451-471.

MacCoun, R. & Reuter, P. (2001). *Drug war heresies: Learning from other vices, times, and places*. Cambridge: Cambridge University Press.

Naylor, R.T. (2004). The underworld of ivory. *Crime Law & Social Change*, 42: 261-295.

Nye, J. (2004). *Soft power: The means to success in world politics*. New York: Public Affairs.

Percipalle, M. et al. (2011). Salmonella infection in illegally imported Spur-Thighed tortoises (Testudo graeca). *Zoonoses and Public Health*, 58: 262-269.

Phelps, J., Carrasco, L.R., & Webb, E.L. (2013). A framework for assessing supply-side wildlife conservation. *Conservation Biology*, 28: 244-257.

Pires, S.F. & Moreto, W.D. (2011). Preventing wildlife crimes: solutions that can overcome the tragedy of the commons. *European Journal on Criminal Policy Research*, 17: 101-123.

Rosen, G.E. & Smith, K.F. (2010). Summarizing the evidence on the international trade in illegal wildlife. *Ecohealth*, 7(24): 24-32.

Sebele, L.S. (2010). Community-based tourism ventures, benefits and challenges: Khama Rhino Sanctuary Trust, Central District, Botswana. *Tourism Management*, 31: 136-146.

Seidensticker, J. (2010). Saving wild tigers: A case study in biodiversity loss and challenges to be met for recovery beyond 2010. *Interactive Zoology*, 5: 285-299.

Singh, S. (2008). Contesting moralities: The politics of wildlife trade in Laos. *Journal of Political Ecology*, 15: 1-20.

Schneider, J.L. (2008). Reducing the illicit trade in endangered wildlife: The market reduction approach. *Journal of Contemporary Criminal Justice*, 24(3): 274-295.

South, N. & Wyatt, T. (2011). Comparing illicit trades in wildlife and drugs: An exploratory study. *Deviant Behavior*, 32(6): 538-561.

Stoett, P. (2002). The international regulation of trade in wildlife: Institutional and normative considerations. *International Environment Agreements: Politics, Law and Economics*, 2: 195-210.

Tisdell, C., Nantha, H.S. & Wilson, C. (2010). Biodiversity conservation and public support for sustainable wildlife harvesting: A case study. *International Journal of Biodiversity Science & Management*, 3(3): 129-144.

Turner, R.L. (2004). Communities, wildlife conservation, and tourism-based development: can community-based nature tourism live up to its promise? *Journal of International Wildlife Law & Policy*, 7(3-4): 161-182.

Von Lampe, K. (2011). The application of the framework of situational crime prevention to 'organised crime'. *Criminology and Criminal Justice*, 11(2): 145-163.

Wasser, S.K. et al. (2004). Assigning African elephant DNA to geographic region of origin: Applications to the ivory trade. *PNAS*, 101(41): 14847-14852.

Wasser, S.K. et al. (2008). Combating the illegal trade in African elephant ivory with DNA forensics. *Conservation Biology*, 22(4): 1065-1071.

Warchol, G.L. (2007). The transnational illegal wildlife trade. *Criminal Justice Studies: A Critical Journal of Crime, Law and Society*, 17(1): 57-73.

Wyatt, T. (2011). The illegal trade raptors in the Russian Federation. *Contemporary Justice Review: Issues in Criminal, Social, and Restorative Justice*, 14(2): 103-123.

Wyatt, T. (2009). Exploring the organization of Russia Far East's illegal wildlife trade: Two case studies of the illegal fur and illegal falcon trades. *Global Crime*, 10(1-2): 144-154.

Yi-Ming et al. (2000). Illegal wildlife trade in the Himalayan region of China. *Biodiversity and Conservation*, 9: 901-918.

Yu, X. (2010). Biodiversity conservation in China: Barriers and future actions. *International Journal of Environmental Studies*, 67(2): 117-126.

3

Wildlife Trafficking in Australia, New Zealand and the United Kingdom: A Comparative Analysis

Tanya Wyatt, Northumbria University, UK

Introduction

Environmental crime, particularly in the transnational context, is an area of global growing concern. Yet throughout the world it has remained outside of the research agenda of academia and research organizations. That has begun to change as is evident by the Australian Research Council funded Transnational Environmental Crime (TEC) Project that this study contributes to. As part of the larger aim of the TEC Project 'to advance our understanding of the ways in which environmental commodities that are either sourced illegally or destined for illegal markets are traded' (Elliott, 2011), this study seeks to explore in more depth wildlife that is illegally trafficked. Also in furtherance of the aims of the project to develop a 'more nuanced, evidence-based understanding of modalities and patterns' of TEC and 'to identify similarities and differences between the criminal practices and markets' (Elliott, 2011), this study adopts a comparative approach incorporating illegal trade data obtained from the Convention on the International Trade in Endangered Species of Wild Fauna and Flora (CITES) online trade database. Rather than comparing wildlife trafficking with another environmental black market, this study compares the nature and extent of wildlife trafficking between Australia, New Zealand, and the United Kingdom (UK). This will further understanding of the geographic differences, which can then inform efforts to improve policy intervention and prevention strategies.

Wildlife is defined within this study in the broadest sense. It includes plants and animals from the entire range of genera and species which are wild and sometimes propagated or captive bred and any products created from these species. Whilst there is legal and illegal trade of commercial and non-commercial species as well as unprotected and protected species, this study focuses on the illegal international trade, or trafficking, of CITES-listed species. This is in part because of the availability of data for CITES species and because CITES is the most prominent and widely adopted mechanism for those protecting endangered and threatened species that are traded internationally. This focus means that the international illegal trade of non-CITES species is not discussed here. The data presented below are the known number of incidents of illegality that are reported to CITES. The total volume and individual amount of wildlife is not detailed as discussed shortly. As with all crimes, the data here is what is known; there is undoubtedly more illegal incidents occurring that are not uncovered or reported. A further note regarding the data – it is not possible to determine if the trends witnessed are due to increased or decreased enforcement efforts, an increase or decrease in illegal activity, or some combination.

The paper begins by detailing the methodology used in collecting data. This is followed by a section on each of the countries that are being compared, which includes discussions of the nature and extent of the wildlife trafficking taking place to and from that country as well as the routes of smuggling and the actors who might be involved. An analysis section exploring the similarities and differences between the countries comes next, followed by some final thoughts.

Methods

Australia, New Zealand, and the UK were chosen for this comparative study as they are culturally and demographically similar with a significant shared history. All three countries are a majority white European with smaller groups ethnic minorities the largest of which is the Maori in New Zealand at 14 per cent (CIA, 2014). The largest religious group in each country is Christian and a vast majority of people speak English as their first language (CIA, 2014). All are islands with a degree of isolation that leads to a level of control of legal and illegal wildlife trade not available to other nations. This allows more equal comparisons of the features of wildlife trafficking, particularly import/export regulations and biodiversity. A review of the relevant literature was supplemented with collection of all illegal trades reported to CITES for each of the three countries from 1975 through 2010. The quantitative trade data was obtained from the CITES website which is maintained by the United Nations Environment Program's Wildlife Conservation Monitoring Centre. All 178 Parties to CITES are required to report all CITES transactions to the Secretariat in Geneva and this is compiled into a publicly available database.

Seven parameters can be searched in the trade database. One of these parameters is 'source' and the selection chosen for this research was 'I' indicating that the wildlife was illegal and has most likely been confiscated or seized. This search term then captures all reported illegal trades for each of the three countries for the entire history of CITES. This data was downloaded into an Excel spread sheet and filters were added to determine trends in the amount of illegal trade overall, countries illegally importing and exporting to the three focus countries, and the species involved. The data contained here is the number of incidents reported and not the number of specimens or the weight of specimens that were illegal. This method was chosen to try to impose some consistency of measuring unit across the data. This is necessary because the format of CITES trade data is quite inconsistent and ranges from individual units, to kilograms, to grams, to pounds, to tons, to tones. Whilst the illegal wildlife was probably confiscated or seized, the CITES data does not give this kind of information; therefore the number of incidents are reported. The intention is to gain insight into the overall trends, geographic patterns and species targeted as well as the type of products that are being smuggled. The latter gives an indication of the reason for the demand, such as use in traditional medicine or as an addition to a collection (Wyatt, 2012). Some brief background will now be given before the findings are presented.

Background

Whilst wildlife trafficking is beginning to receive much needed attention from the academic community (see Schneider, 2012; Wyatt, 2012), studies are still limited as to the regional variations that exist as well as the legal, social, and cultural factors influencing this crime. This research aims to fill part of the gap in knowledge by exploring the regional differences in wildlife trafficking between Australia, New Zealand, and the UK.

A brief survey of wildlife trafficking in these nations reveals differences in trafficking levels and the approaches to combat it. With a high amount of biodiversity and endemism, Australia allows no export of native live wildlife and has low amounts of detected illegal trade; New Zealand is equally high in biodiversity and endemism, allows the regulated export of wildlife, and has the highest amount of detected illegal trade of the three; and the UK, on the other hand, has comparatively low biodiversity, allows the regulated export of wildlife, and also has somewhat high amounts of wildlife trafficking (see Figure 1). As mentioned earlier, these three countries are demographically similar with a significant shared cultural history, so presumably the differences in levels of wildlife trafficking stem from law enforcement tactics, the import/export regulations, or some as yet unidentified correlating factor(s).

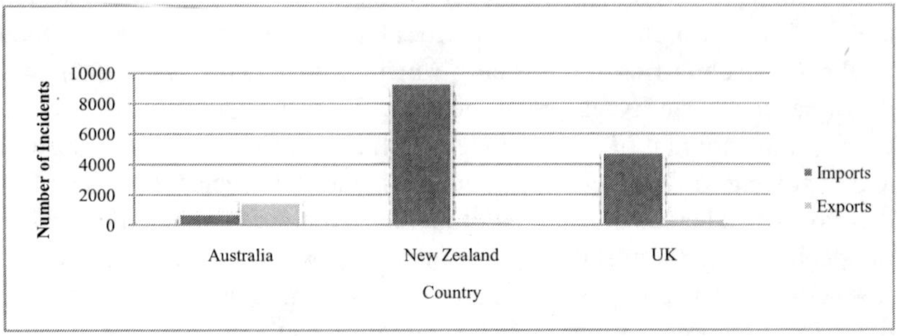

Figure 1: Illegal CITES Imports and Exports 1980-2010

In terms of regulation, Australia and the UK both joined CITES in 1976, so are early adopters of provisions to protect wildlife under this framework. New Zealand did not become a signatory until 1989. Reporting trade data to the Secretariat started in earnest for the three countries at different times, which is evident in the sections below, but from Figure 1 it is clear that the first data became available in 1980. As Parties of CITES, each country has created a Management Authority which oversees the permit system attached to trading the differently listed species. Appendix I species can only be traded in limited circumstances and require both an import and export permit. Appendix II species are subject to trade quotas and monitored so that trade does not threaten that species' survival in the wild. These transactions need an export permit although a country can be more strict than the CITES standard. Each country also creates a Scientific Authority, which advises on what level quotas should be set and on the health and viability of species populations.

The Standing Committee of CITES establishes Categories indicating the degree of implementation of the legislation required to enforce CITES provisions. In Category 1 the country generally meets the requirements, in Category 2 some of the legislation does and does not meet the standard, and in Category 3 the legislation does not meet the standards. Australia, New Zealand, and the UK are all Category 1 countries. An additional administrative layer exists in the UK in that it has 11 overseas dependent territories in which the proper legislation must also be implemented. Three territories are in Category 1, six in Category 2, and two in Category 3 (CITES, 2012), so attention needs to be paid to further implementation of CITES in UK territories. New Zealand has three associated territories, two of which are self-governing and therefore responsible for CITES themselves. Neither the Cook Islands nor Niue are signatories to CITES. This may in fact create a loophole for smuggling, which is explored below. The specific legislation that complies with CITES is detailed in the next country-specific sections as are the individual trends that are evident in each of these locales.

Australia

Australia is one of the 25 biodiversity hotspots in the world, which indicates that there is a high number of native species. In this case, endemic species are estimated to make up 80 per cent of the fauna and flora of this island continent (Alacs and Georges, 2008). Such uniqueness is often tied to wildlife trafficking where collectors in particular seek out less common species. Wildlife trafficking is especially a cause for concern for such environments because of the threat it poses to bio-security. This threat includes the introduction of parasites, viruses, and invasive species, all of which can have devastating consequences for endemic species (Alacs and Georges, 2008). This is strikingly evident in Australian history with the introduction of the rabbit and the cane toad. Both animals have caused significant damage – the rabbit to the native plants and thus unique ecosystems, and the cane toad to the native animals by out-competing them and poisoning predators not evolved to coexist with cane toads.

Research by Rosen and Smith (2010) shows that between 1996 and 2008, 6 per cent of recorded global illegal wildlife seizures occurred in Australia. This is equal to the amount seized in the US, and behind the UK (10 per cent), China (11 per cent), and India (20 per cent). Other studies by Halstead (1994), and Alacs and Georges (2008), provide foundational information into the nature and extent of wildlife trafficking in Australia. Combining this with CITES trade data, a current picture of the scope and scale is able to be pieced together. Halstead's (1994) study focused on the federal and state legislation that pertained to trade in wildlife. Whilst much of this has undergone revision, there are still relevant elements in her discussion that will be mentioned here. Alacs and Georges (2008) gained access to the Australian Customs' database of wildlife prosecutions from 1994 to 2007. This not only provides information as to the trends of wildlife trafficking, but also data as to the response of enforcement agencies to violations.

CITES in Australia is complied with through the Environmental Protection and Biodiversity Conservation Act 1999. This piece of legislation addresses more than wildlife trade and provides a foundation for preservation of ecological communities and heritage sites as well as implementing sustainable practices throughout industries that impact upon the environment. The Department of Sustainability, Environment, Water, Population and Communities (DSEWPaC) oversees the CITES permit system, which pertains of course to international trade. Wildlife trafficking related violations can also be prosecuted under State legislation. This adds a layer of complexity to the Australian context because there are variations of licensing, enforcement, and sentencing of offences between states and territories. This provides a means for organised and international trafficking to utilize differences in state regulations to aid them in smuggling (Halstead, 1994).

Export of live wildlife is essentially prohibited (Alacs and Georges, 2008). Therefore legal commercial operations must gain government approval and there is a licensing system for these businesses or individuals. This also consists of a strictly regulated permit system mainly for fisheries, crocodile farms, native flora collecting and growing, and kangaroo meat from sanctioned harvests. Captive breeding of native birds may provide a means of laundering wild-caught birds. Imports also need approval, even CITES Appendix II species, which is stricter than the convention requirements. Non-commercial imports and exports all need permits – so trade for pets, personal use, research, exhibition, and education are all tightly controlled as well (Alacs and Georges, 2008; Halstead, 1994).

Smuggling is typically accomplished through human couriers and postal deliveries (Bricknell, 2010). Therefore, wildlife trafficking is mostly detected at airports and in the post, with raids associated with these investigations also uncovering information (Alacs and Georges, 2008). Whilst Australian Customs and Border Protection Services is the main agency tasked with uncovering wildlife trafficking, the Australian Federal Police, DSEWPaC, and the Department of Agriculture, Fisheries and Forestry also play roles in investigations and prosecutions. Customs adopts a risk-assessment strategy for inspection priority, so search a limited number of people and packages either randomly or based upon intelligence (Australian Customs, 2010). In contrast, DSEWPaC relies on self-regulation and voluntary compliance schemes (Horne, 2013b). DSEWPaC deals with post-border possession and trafficking of wildlife and focuses their attention on links to organised crime (DSEWPaC, 2010; Horne, 2013b). One per cent of Customs' seizures are 'major' in terms of quantity and value. The vast majority are people bringing in prohibited items purchased at international markets (Alacs and Georges, 2008). DSEWPaC has tried to address this aspect by providing travel agents with educational information about wildlife trafficking to try to curb tourists unintentionally buying products from endangered and protected species (Horne, 2013b). Bricknell (2010) categorizes the illegal activity as consisting of illegal export of native species, illegal import of exotic species, and the illegal domestic breeding and trading of both native and exotic species. This is explored further in analyzing the CITES data.

There was an increase in the number of Customs' seizures from 3,904 in 2004-2005 to 7,533 in 2006-2007, perhaps because of increased screening at airports, indicating more success at detection rather than an increase in trafficking. Some of the major seizures involved organised crime networks, which have been implicated in wildlife trade in Australia (Alacs and Georges, 2008). There is anecdotal evidence that reptile and insect trade involves outlaw motorcycle gangs (Blindell, 2006). More concrete proof is seen in incidents, which included trafficking of pythons and birds, powdered seahorse from China through Australia to New Zealand, and cycads and orchids involving the US, South Africa, and Zimbabwe (Alacs and Georges, 2008). Research by the International Fund for Animal Welfare (IFAW, 2008) found Internet sales of CITES II species in Australia, particularly of the *Hoodia* plant for weight loss and some ivory. Overall the seizures are mostly of reptiles, which are smuggled through the post, inside ornaments, toys, books, or computers, and in socks, cigarette boxes, and specially built clothing (Alacs and Georges, 2008).

The next most commonly seized wildlife is birds and eggs. There are also a significant amount of illegal imports of what Alacs and Georges (2008) refer to as 'complementary' medicines from endangered species, which are used in traditional Asian or Chinese medicines. DSEWPaC has worked with the Australian Acupuncture and Chinese Medicine Association to develop a certification scheme that will reduce the use of endangered and protected species (Horne, 2013b). Other seizures consist of exports of native flora, imports of exotic fish, and confiscation of insects, arthropods, coral, and ivory (Alacs and Georges, 2008). In general, the perpetrators are a mixture of Australians and foreign nationals. There is also a mix of people acting alone or in small semi-organised groups, but both of these are more prevalent than more serious organised crime groups (Bricknell, 2010). The Customs seizures data does not reflect the concern in Australia over illegal, unregulated, and unreported fishing, which is degrading fish stocks particularly on the north coast (Putt and Anderson, 2007). Nor does the data capture the amount of illegal timber that enters Australia, which is also a large part of wildlife trafficking. Australia plays a role as a consumer of illegal timber and as of 2012 had passed the Illegal Logging Prohibition Act 2012 (Parliament of Australia, 2012), that bans the importation and sale of all timber products from illegally sourced wood similar to legislation in both the European Union (EU) and the US.

Turning to the CITES trade data, similar information is obtained in regard to species. Australia has the least number of illegal imports of wildlife in this comparative study with only 728 incidents over 30 years. Figure 2 provides a break-down of the species most frequently illegally imported. These appear to fulfil the demand for traditional medicines (seahorses, costus, and ginseng) as well as collectors' items and pets (ivory, snakes, and tortoises). In contrast, and most likely stemming from its high biodiversity, Australia had the highest amount of illegal exports (1,506), yet the CITES trade data reveals a slightly different trend in illegality than is reported in the literature. In terms of incidents, reptiles, particularly crocodiles, are the most frequently smuggled wildlife from Australia, which corresponds to previous studies. While the commentary literature raises concerns over birds, the CITES trade data indicates that corals are the next most frequent illegal export (see Figure 3). If other marine species are added, such as giant clams, conchs, and mammals, marine wildlife is trafficked nearly as frequently as reptiles. This seems to indicate that a re-evaluation is needed of what is considered high-risk wildlife in the context of regulation and enforcement.

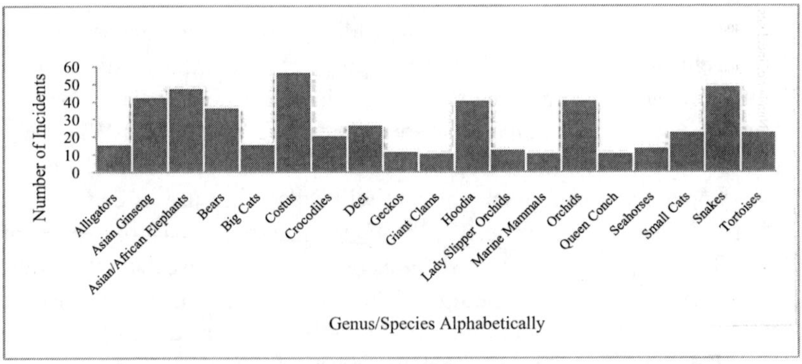

Figure 2: Australia Illegal CITES Imports by Species 1988-2010

The CITES trade data collected provides the trends of a longer period of time than that from the study by Alacs and Georges (2008) and also

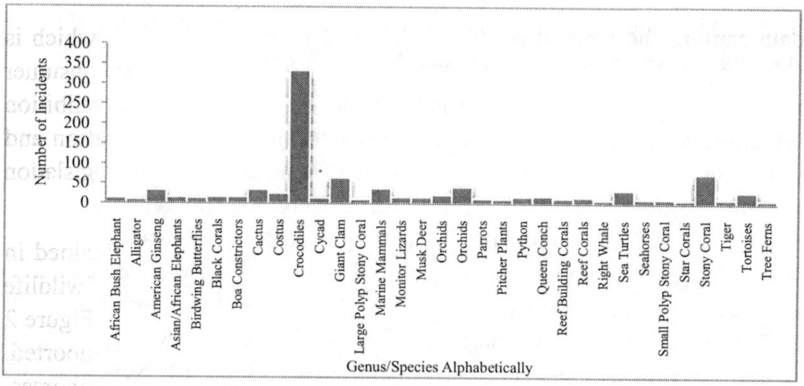

Figure 3: Australia Illegal CITES Exports by Species 1982-2010

identifies the countries involved in these illegal transactions. Although Australia was an early signatory to CITES, the data for illegal imports does not start until 1988, presumably indicating there was no detected illegal activity that needed to be reported in the early 1980s, not that there was no wildlife trafficking (see Figure 4). This assumption is supported in the illegal export data, which starts in 1982 (see Figure 4). As mentioned previously, Australia has relatively few illegal imports and according to the CITES data a majority of these occurred in 2009 with others taking place in the

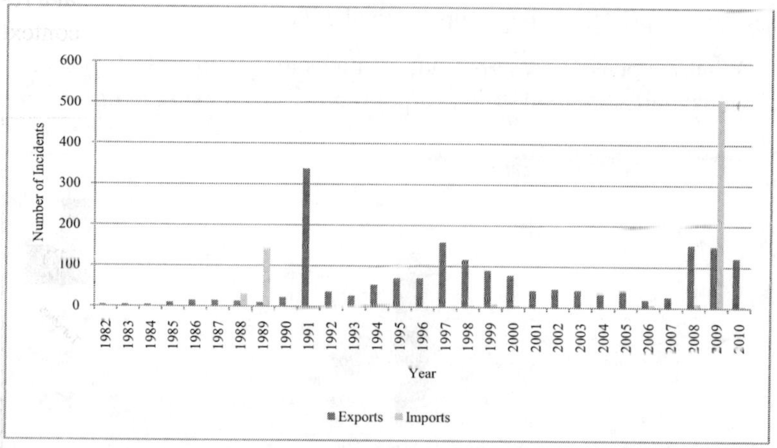

Figure 4: Australia Illegal CITES Exports and Imports 1982-2010

late 1980s. Illegal exports fluctuate over the data period with the peak year being 1991. Whilst there is no clear pattern of increase or decrease, it can be noted that the final three years of data, 2008 to 2010, are three out of the five highest years for illegal exports in the 28 years of data.

In addition to dividing the data by year, Figures 5 and 6 show the breakdown of which countries were involved in the illegal transactions with Australia. The destinations of illegal exports from Australia were predominantly to New Zealand followed closely by exports to the US (see Figure 5). The UK also features in the illegal exports, but to a significantly lesser degree. The countries listed are all those that were collected in the data. This indicates that Europe is also a destination for illegal exports as well as Japan, Singapore, and South Africa. This is significantly different to the origin of illegal imports to Australia (see Figure 6). New Zealand, the US, and the UK again feature in the illegal imports, but the other countries are those, like Australia, with high levels of biodiversity. For instance, several Southeast Asian nations are implicated, such as Indonesia, Malaysia, and Thailand. China, Taiwan, and Hong Kong also have incidents of sending illegal imports to Australia. Of note is that two Pacific Island nations are involved – New Caledonia and Vanuatu – and for the highest amount of illegality (81 incidents).It is unknown where the illegal wildlife originated. From examination of the illegal imports, it can be seen that there is a regional pattern to the confiscation, where a majority of the illegality is stemming from neighbouring nations or those within reasonably close proximity. This is in contrast to the exports, which, except for New Zealand, are predominantly going to the US and Europe.

What happens to these offenders? Fines are up to A$110,000 for an individual and A$550,000 for a corporation with a maximum of ten years

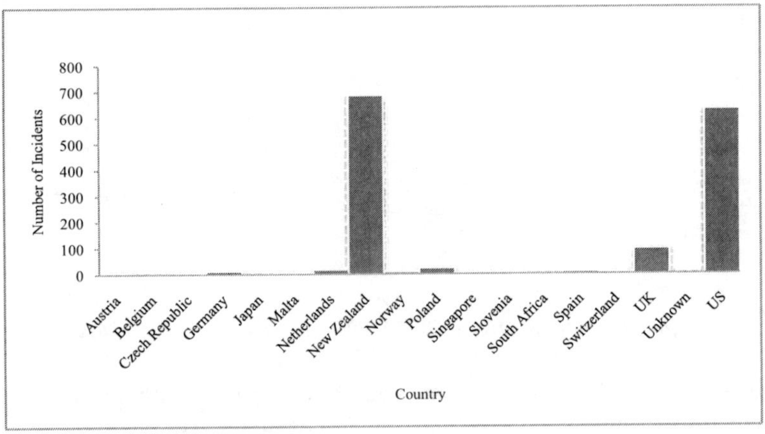

Figure 5: Destination of Australian IIlegal CITES Exports 1982-2010

imprisonment. Alacs and Georges (2008) claim that this is fairly severe compared to other countries. Fines are the most common penalty and are less than the value of the wildlife on the black market. Sentence severity has increased, but prosecutions remain less than one-quarter of identified cases, so while harsher in principle, in practice penalties appear rather weak (Alacs and Georges, 2008). Bricknell (2010) also observed that penalties are only a fraction of the maximum that could be given.

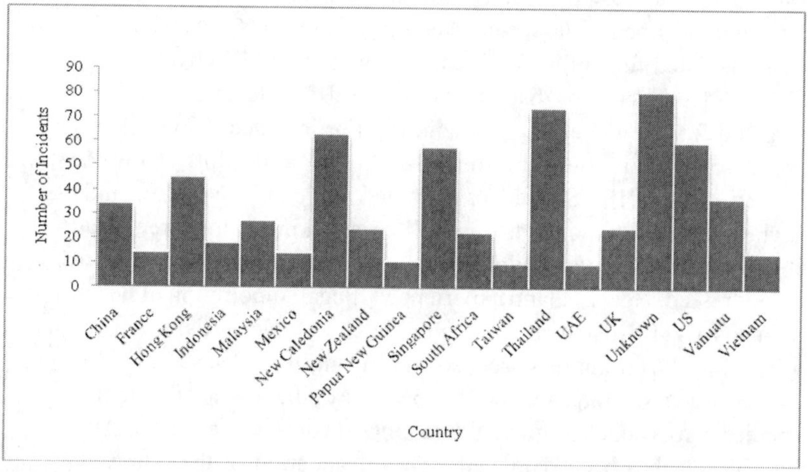

Figure 6: Origin of Australian Illegal CITES Imports 1988-2010

In an effort to protect its highly diverse ecology, Australia has opted for comparatively stringent regulation of wildlife trade in and out of its borders. Previous studies and the CITES trade data on illegality indicate that this has possibly been a successful strategy in terms of limiting the amount of wildlife trafficking that is taking place. This cannot be known for certain since there is no way of knowing how much illegal trade is occurring that is not discovered. Whilst there are incidents, as will be clear from the next two sections, the known incidents in Australia at least are not on the same scale as those experienced by other similar countries. It is possible that the lack of wildlife trafficking is influenced by the severe penalties that can (although as yet have not been) be given were someone to be convicted of smuggling plants or animals. What could be happening and would not be captured within this data set is domestic trafficking. There is the possibility of Australian inter-state smuggling of protected species that may be contributing to their decline, which may warrant detailed examination at the state level. As was clear from the data above, there is a connection between Australia and New Zealand in regard to wildlife trafficking. New Zealand's efforts to control the illegal trade are the focus of the next section.

New Zealand

Whereas wildlife trafficking has received a reasonable amount of attention in Australia (Halstead, 1994; Alacs and Georges, 2008; Bricknell, 2010), a literature search for similar studies in New Zealand found very little. This is a cause for concern for two reasons. First, New Zealand has a large number of endemic species stemming from the North and South Islands being isolated for millions of years (New Zealand Biodiversity, no date). This uniqueness means that many of the bird, reptile, and insect species are targeted for the illegal trade in wildlife. For instance, 16 jewelled geckos were seized and thought to be worth NZ$200,000 (New Zealand Government, 2010). Second, as indicated in Figure 1, New Zealand has the highest number of incidents of wildlife trafficking of the three countries in this comparative study, which is evidence of criminal activity that needs to be addressed. New Zealand experienced illegal importation of nearly twice as many CITES-listed species as the UK, and over ten times as many as Australia. Illegal imports are also significant in the New Zealand context, as they are in Australia and the UK, because of the risk and threat of invasive species that is attached to the illegal imports of wildlife. Just as Australia's biodiversity has been damaged from introduction of the rabbit and cane toad, New Zealand's ecosystems have suffered from possums, cats, dogs, and so on. Thirty-two per cent of endemic land and fresh-water based birds on the islands have become extinct, as have three reptile species and 11 vascular plants (New Zealand Biodiversity, n.d). Within the last few years, *varroa* mites were introduced when someone smuggled in a queen bee (New Zealand Government, 2010). This can have devastating consequences for the agricultural industry. There is a sense of urgency to protect the remaining biodiversity, and stopping both the illegal import and export of wildlife may play a role in doing so.

As mentioned earlier, New Zealand became a signatory to CITES in 1989, over a decade after it was established. The piece of legislation that meets compliance with the requirements set out by CITES is the Trade in Endangered Species Act 1989. CITES enforcement is mainly carried out by the Department of Conservation as the Management Authority, although New Zealand Customs and the Ministry of Primary Industries also play roles. These three have signed a memorandum of agreement to form the Wildlife Enforcement Group (WEG) which focuses on enforcement and capacity-building. The Customs service hosts WEG as well as providing resources and staff, as do the Department of Conservation and the Ministry of Agriculture and Forestry (New Zealand Government, 2010). WEG was the first cooperation of its kind and is often cited as the possible model for proactive intelligence gathering to uncover modus operandi and tackle future crimes (Horne, 2013b).

Most well documented regarding the illegal wildlife trade in New Zealand is the illegal export of birds. Australia banned export of its native species in 1960, which resulted in an increase in prices of Australian species, particularly birds. As reported by TRAFFIC Oceania, bird traffickers began smuggling birds from Australia to New Zealand on light planes and in specially built clothing. Networks with traffickers from Australia, New Zealand, the US, the UK, and South Africa were using New Zealand's captive-bred industry to launder wild-caught native Australian species and then transport them 'legally' out of New Zealand to other parts of the globe. At the time, the government was criticized that the Trade in Endangered Species Act 1989 was flawed and allowed this sort of laundering to take place. These networks were not serious organised crime, only loose affiliations (Holden, 1997), but there have been cases where serious organised crime has been implicated in wildlife trafficking in New Zealand (New Zealand Government, 2010). Whilst the New Zealand government claims organised crimes' involvement in overfishing, wildlife trafficking, and illegal logging are well-documented, most evidence is anecdotal. Exceptions to this are such cases in New Zealand where gangs and Asian organised crime have been arrested for poaching *paua* (edible sea snails known elsewhere as abalone) and rock lobster, which were estimated to be worth NZ$270,000 in a year (New Zealand Government, 2010).

New Zealand and Australia have a fair amount of overlap in terms of the species which are being trafficked. As seen in Figure 7, reptiles such as crocodiles and sea turtles are also illegally imported into New Zealand. Imports also consist of those products categorized as traditional medicines – ginseng, costus, musk deer, and *saiga*, for instance. Difference is noticeable in that corals are illegally imported to New Zealand whereas they are, as indicated, one of the main illegal exports from Australia. Looking more closely at the data, this is clearly the flow of this illegal market. It cannot be determined if New Zealand is the final destination for the coral or if the country is a transit place for smuggling coral to other destinations. There is also the possibility that this is not an 'organised' smuggling operation, but rather evidence of large amounts of uninformed tourists illegally taking home coral souvenirs. The species that are listed in Figure 8 are only those where there are more than one hundred incidents within the 21-year dataset.

There are hundreds of different species within the total 9,320incidents of illegal imports.

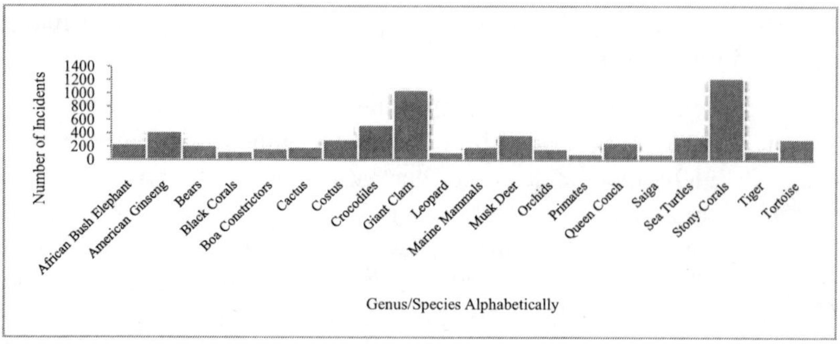

Figure 7: New Zeland Illegal CITES Imports 1989-2010

New Zealand had only 221 illegal exports between 1983 and 2010, the least of the three countries. Presumably, there is export data before New Zealand joined CITES because other Parties were documenting where their illegal imports were originating. Those species with more than five incidents are found in Figure 8. These include some reptiles, but mainly feature marine mammals and corals as well as several plants, including two types of orchids and two types of native ferns. This raises an important point for the study of wildlife trafficking, which will be addressed in the analysis section.

Illegal imports of wildlife to New Zealand fluctuate less than those observed in Australia. There is a clear increase from 1989 to 1998, when there were 902 illegal imports reported to CITES (see Figure 9). Illegal imports steadily declined until 2006. At that point, there is an increase and the last three years of complete data, 2008 to 2010, are fairly consistent at over 500 incidents each year. To put this in perspective, this is more than one confiscation or seizure every day. In terms of exports, there is no distinctive pattern (see Figure 9). The highest number of incidents – 22 – was in 2009, but clearly New Zealand authorities and WEG need to spend their resources and times stopping illegal imports of wildlife from getting into the country. These exports are mostly bound for either the US (124 incidents) or the other countries in this study, Australia and the UK (24 and 34 respectively) (see Figure 10). Illegal imports also involve the US, which is one of the five main origins of illegal wildlife coming to New Zealand (see Figure 11). As was the case in Australia, another of the five main origins is 'unknown' which means that the place where the illegal wildlife was taken from cannot be determined. The three other countries are

Australia, which reflects the pattern of illegal coral trade discussed earlier, China, and Hong Kong. This may account for the illicit trade in traditional medicines that is witnessed coming into New Zealand, which could be connected to the diaspora populations of Northeast Asia. Illegal imports are also coming from countries in Southeast Asia, the Pacific Islands, and Africa. The Cook Islands has 178 incidents of illegal imports into New Zealand. Whilst this may not appear to be significant within the larger picture, for a small self-governed island it raises the question as to why the Cook Islands have not become a party to CITES since there is clearly evidence that wildlife trafficking is taking place there. It may be that the islands are a transhipment point rather than a source, but adoption of CITES would still address this. The diversity of both products and countries that

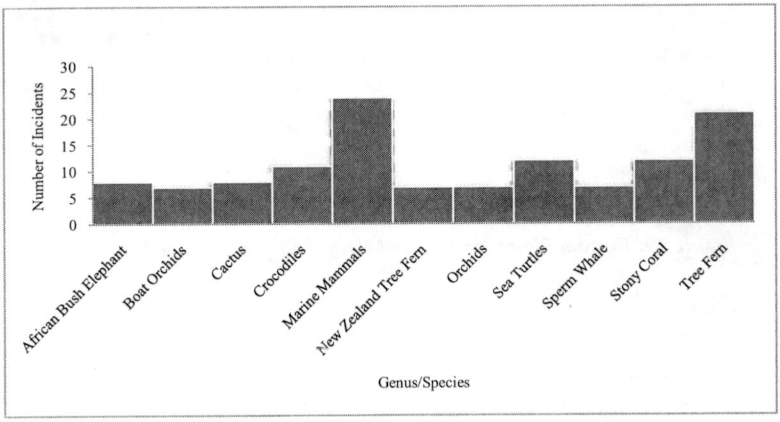

Figure 8: New Zeland IIlegal CITES Exports 1983-2010

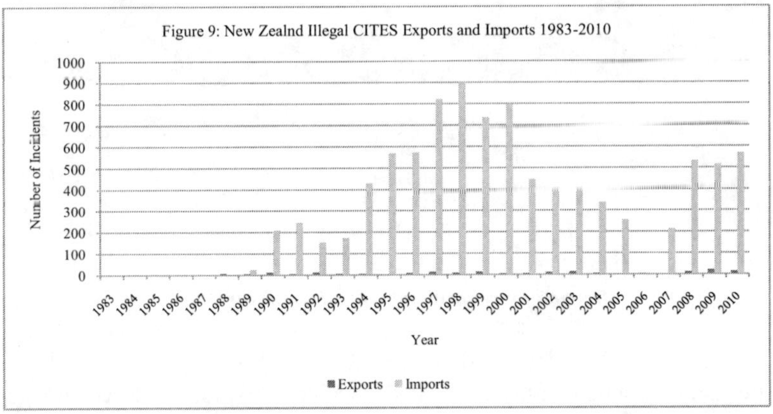

Figure 9: New Zeland IIlegal CITES Exports and Imports 1983-2010

are involved with the trafficking of wildlife into New Zealand gives an idea of the complex task that is given to WEG, Customs, and law enforcement in uncovering this black market.

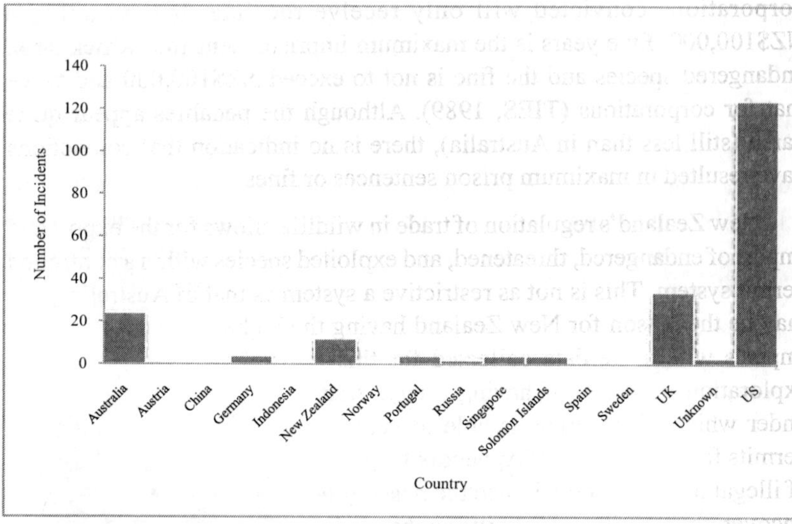

Figure 10: Destination of New Zeland IIlegal CITES Exports 1983-2010

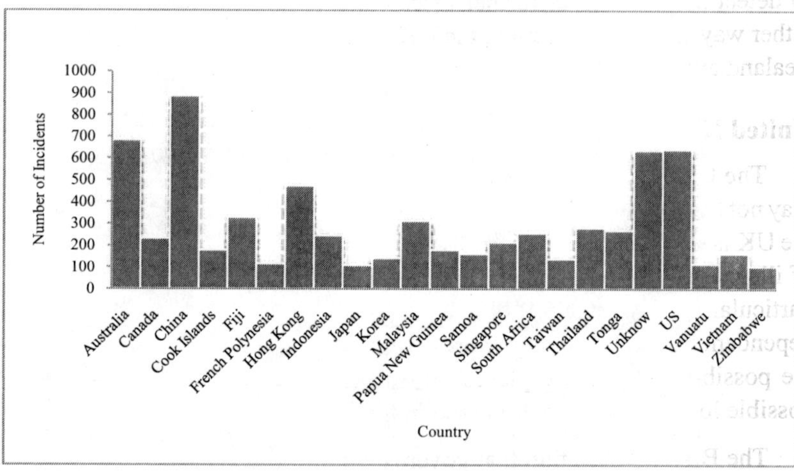

Figure 11: Origin of New Zealand IIlegal CITES Imports 1989-2010

The Trade in Endangered Species Act 1989 has increasing penalties depending on whether the trafficked species is exploited, threatened, or endangered. For conviction of trafficking in exploited species, an individual perpetrator may be given a fine of up to NZ$37,500, whereas a corporation can receive a fine of up to NZ$75,000. Trafficking of threatened species may result in up to three years in prison and a possible NZ$50,000 fine; corporations convicted will only receive the fine, but it could be NZ$100,000. Five years is the maximum imprisonment for trafficking in endangered species and the fine is not to exceed NZ$100,000 and twice that for corporations (TIES, 1989). Although the penalties appear quite harsh (still less than in Australia), there is no indication that convictions have resulted in maximum prison sentences or fines.

New Zealand's regulation of trade in wildlife allows for the export and import of endangered, threatened, and exploited species within a controlled permit system. This is not as restrictive a system as that of Australia. This may be the reason for New Zealand having the highest amount of illegal imports within the data collected for this research. It is worth further exploration to unpick if having a legal trade is providing a mechanism under which illegal trade is able to take place, and if requiring CITES permits for importation of Appendix II species would decrease the amount of illegal imports. There is also the possibility that the specialized WEG is uncovering more illegal activity, so that their success makes it appear as if New Zealand has higher incidents of illegality where in fact they are able to detect more. Without further research, it is not possible to be certain either way. In the next section, the UK context is compared to that of New Zealand and Australia.

United Kingdom

The UK was an earlier signatory to CITES. Whereas the British Isles may not have the diversity of wildlife present in Australia and New Zealand, the UK is still faced with the challenges of preventing a significant amount of illegal wildlife trade. This stems from the UK being a destination for particular categories of wildlife, as detailed shortly. The 11 UK overseas dependent territories contain more diversity than the UK itself and there is the possibility that these places are sources of trafficked wildlife. This possible loophole will be discussed in the analysis.

The British legislation that governs wildlife trafficking and therefore complies with CITES is the Control of Trade in Endangered Species (Enforcement) (Amendment) Regulations 2005 (COTES). As part of the EU, the UK must implement legislation that conforms to EU regulations and COTES does that in terms of wildlife trafficking. COTES prohibits the 'import, export, landing, keeping, transportation and commercial display of, trade in and disposal of flora and fauna (including parts and derivatives)'. This applies when a person has knowledge that the wildlife was illegal and requires that the person make an effort to determine the legality (COTES, 2005). The legislation has Annex A species that are the most endangered and Annex B species that are threatened. This essentially corresponds to the CITES Appendices. The UK Border Agency has a CITES Enforcement Team whose task is to uncover smuggling and there is also the National Wildlife Crime Unit that assists with investigations of smuggling of CITES species. A risk-based approach is also used in the UK when searching for smuggled wildlife. Wildlife that is confiscated is housed at the Heathrow Animal Reception Centre until a suitable permanent home can be found and the reception centre assists the CITES Enforcement Team in searching legal shipments of wildlife that enter the UK's largest port, Heathrow Airport for hidden or stowaway wildlife (Wyatt, 2013).

Wildlife trafficking in the UK has been a research topic both by scholars and non-governmental organisations (see Lowther, Cook and Roberts, 2002; TRAFFIC, 2011; Wyatt, 2013). The patterns that have been observed are similar to those that have been discussed in regards to Australia and New Zealand. All three countries have legal and illegal trade in reptiles for the pet industry. In the UK, reptiles and amphibians have been increasing in popularity with a wider range of species on offer than was observed previously (Altherr and Freyer, 2001). In fact, the number of species for sale more than doubled from 1992-1993 to 2004-2005 with only 31 per cent of the species remaining the same in the time periods analyzed. This has implications for the illegal trade because captive breeding cannot adjust quickly to new demands in the market (Tapley, Griffiths and Bride, 2011), so demand is met by capturing reptiles from the wild.

As Customs seizures collected by TRAFFIC show, reptiles are the wildlife that features most prominently in wildlife trafficking in the UK. Seizures at Heathrow Airport from 1997 to 2011 expose the range of reptile species as well as amphibians. There are numerous snakes, geckos, monitor lizards, salamanders, and frogs (TRAFFIC, 2011). Like Australia and New Zealand, and arguably all countries which are importers of illegal wildlife, unregulated wildlife trafficking may be a conduit by which non-human animal disease is spread. For instance in the UK, the spread of Bactrachochytrium dendrobatidis (a fatal skin disease causing multiple amphibian extinctions) is linked to the trade in frogs (Fisher and Garner, 2007). Birds are also smuggled into the UK for the pet industry, as with Australia and New Zealand (TRAFFIC, 2011). This seizure data is of CITES-listed species, so is also contained within the CITES trade data collected for this study, but it is only part of a larger picture discussed below. Perpetrators of wildlife trafficking in the UK also fit a similar profile to those in Australia and New Zealand. Whilst organised crime appears to be playing an increasing role in smuggling of wildlife (Lowther, Cook and Roberts, 2002), a vast majority of the offenders are individuals with some connections to loosely connected informal networks.

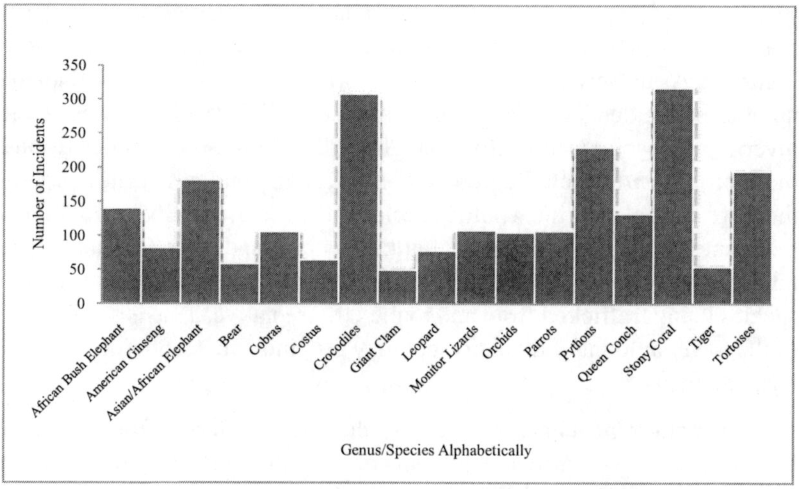

Figure 12: UK Illegal CITES Imports by Species 1980-2010

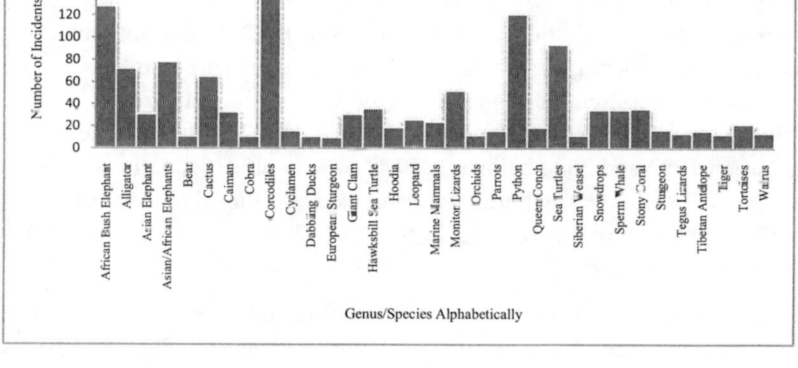

Figure 13: UK Illegal CITES Exports by Species 1982-2010

Despite being some 19,000 kms apart, the UK has a similar pattern of wildlife trafficking to that of Australia and New Zealand in terms of species smuggled. The illegal imports from 1980 to 2010 are not unlike those in the two previous sections: reptiles (cobras, crocodiles, lizards, and tortoises), birds (parrots), marine wildlife (coral, conch, and giant clams), traditional medicines (ginseng and costus) and ivory are the most frequently found species (see Figure 12). Figure 12 does not include the entire range of species, only those with over 50 recorded incidents. Over the 30-year period there have been 4,762 incidents of illegal imports reported to CITES (see Figure 1). As in New Zealand, illegal exports are significantly less than the number of incidents of illegal importation (see Figure 13). However, the diversity of species is not unlike that of the illegal imports. Reptiles feature most prominently including crocodiles, pythons, and sea turtles. Again, there are multiple marine wildlife species and those used to make traditional medicines. What is notable is that unlike Australia and New Zealand, where many of the species being trafficked are native, very few if any of the species being trafficked from and to the UK are native. This is a reflection of the lower amount of diversity, but may also indicate laundering through legal channels.

The pattern of illegal imports into the UK is different from the other two countries. No significant amounts of illegal imports into the UK were reported to CITES until 1997 (see Figure 14). In the period to 2004, there are more than 250 incidents each year at a minimum. The levels then fluctuate until 2010. It is only possible to speculate as to the reasons for this pattern. It is possible that enforcement and detection efforts were improved in the late 1990s and that this enabled the UK to uncover more illegal wildlife trade and to have more to report to CITES. The increase corresponds to the first drafting of COTES in 1997, so possibly there is a connection to increased law enforcement attention. This is arguably more probable than a significant increase in the amount of trafficking occurring. Illegal exports are reported every year from 1982 with the time period between 1997 and 2004 being relatively high to other years. In contrast to illegal imports, illegal exports have remained at the level of the early 2000s with 2009 being the second highest (127 incidents) since CITES implementation (see Figure 14).

Illegal exports from the UK are going to fewer countries than seen above (see Figure 15). Predominantly, species are sent to the US and New Zealand, with a few being bound for Australia. The US is also the most frequent importer of illegally traded wildlife although 'unknown' has a higher number of incidents (see Figure 19). Australia is one of the origin

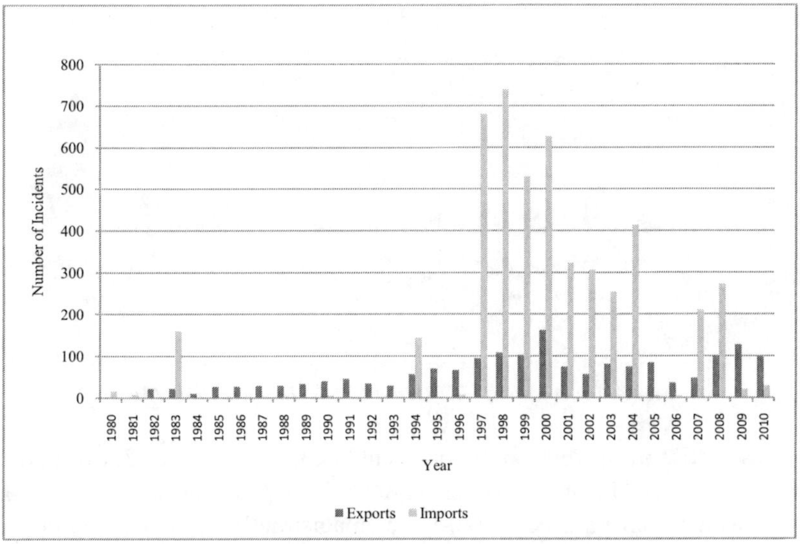

Figure 14: UK Illegal CITES Exports and Imports 1980-2010

countries of illegal imports with over 40 incidents. New Zealand had fewer than 40, so does not appear on the figure. The countries are in every region of the world – South America, the Caribbean, Asia, Africa, Europe, and Oceania. Apart from the US, China, Thailand, and South Africa stand out as countries which are regular origins of illegal imports. That being said, Figure 16 shows many countries that may warrant particular scrutiny of their wildlife trading.

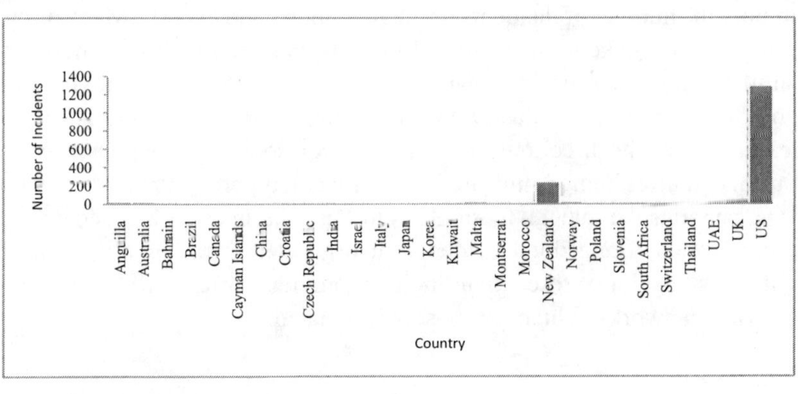

Figure 15: Destination of UK Illegal CITES Exports 1982-2010

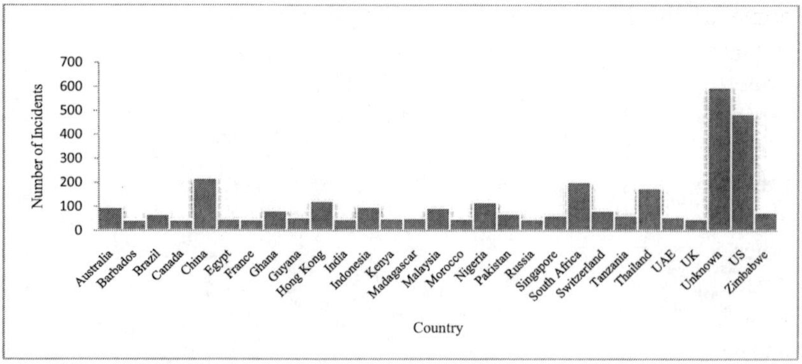

Figure 16: Origin of UK Illegal CITES Imports 1980-2010

Wildlife traffickers can be prosecuted either under COTES or under the Customs and Excise Management Act (1979) (Alacs and Georges, 2008). The former can be tried in the lower magistrate's court. If a summary conviction is found then the perpetrator may be given up to six months in prison and/or a fine of up to £5,000 or both. A COTES violation can also be tried in the Crown court where a conviction on indictment may result in up to five years in prison and/or unlimited fines or both (COTES, 2005). If convicted for a violation of the Customs and Excise Management Act (1979), a perpetrator can receive a maximum of seven years imprisonment and unlimited fines (Alacs and Georges, 2008). As seen in the previous two countries, maximum penalties are never given and cases rarely go to the higher court (Lowther, Cook and Roberts, 2002).

The UK falls within the middle of three countries studied here in terms of both the number of incidents of illegal imports and exports. Many of the same species make up these illegal imports and exports, which indicates similar wildlife consumer demands to Australia and New Zealand: reptiles and birds for the pet industry and traditional medicines. There is illegal trade between the three countries, and the UK also contends with numerous origin countries being implicated in the illegal imports. In regards to who is perpetrating the smuggling, similarly to Australia and New Zealand, whilst there is mostly anecdotal evidence of organised crime involvement in wildlife smuggling, prosecutions indicate individual offenders acting within informal networks, which are loosely associated.

Analysis

In general, Australia, New Zealand, and the UK have a fair amount in common when it comes to wildlife trafficking. In 2010, each country had some of the highest amount of illegal exports recorded since the implementation of CITES. Australia had a low number of incidents of illegal imports in 2010, but the number of incidents is usually low. The UK's reported incidents were also down, but New Zealand saw a high number of illegal imports. As four of the six measurements of trade (import and export for each of the three countries) are relatively high, this indicates that wildlife smuggling continues to warrant attention in these countries. Each of the other countries features in the illegal imports and exports of one another – Australia receives and sends illegal wildlife to the UK and New Zealand; New Zealand receives and sends illegal wildlife to the UK and Australia; and the UK receives and sends illegal wildlife to Australia and New Zealand (the latter does not appear in Figure 11 because of the comparatively low amount). Efforts to reduce illegal wildlife trade may then entail closer cooperation between the three countries.

Other countries that should be involved and that are included in each of the three countries dataset are the US, China, Hong Kong, Thailand, and South Africa to name just those with a significant number of incidents. Other Southeast Asian and European countries could also have an impact. It is noticeable that each country has a high number of illegal incidents for which the origin is unknown. This indicates that countries which allow the export of wildlife must be called upon to monitor exports much more strictly as they leave the source country. This may reduce the amount of illegal imports to other countries, but also enable the wildlife to be returned to the place where it was captured from or at least remain in the country from which it was taken.

The species that are illegally smuggled in the three countries also tend to be similar. There is clearly an illegal market for pets, both reptiles and birds, in Australia, New Zealand, and the UK. The CITES data does not actually indicate a high amount of bird trafficking in relation to New Zealand although the literature has documented it in the past (TRAFFIC, 2011). The pet industry raises regulatory challenges because, as indicated in each of the above sections, part of the demand is reliant upon captive breeding programmes. Captive breeding provides a means to launder wild-caught reptiles and birds into the legitimate market. Although captive breeding has been advocated as a means to reduce the pressure on wild species, this does not always happen for a variety of reasons. Intensive captive breeding takes place from a limited gene pool, which can mean low fitness levels of the progeny produced – this ultimately leads to hobbyists still seeking wild-caught specimens because they are healthier. Also, captive breeding satiates the demand, thus decreasing prices and the incentive to captive breed

(Tapley, Griffiths and Bride, 2011), so wildlife are still taken from their natural habitats. Also, when one species is regulated it often displaces the demand to another species, which may not be captive bred (Carpenter et al., 2004). So whilst captive breeding may help to some degree, it has not completely reduced the pressure on wildlife being captured. This is important because it is part of the regulatory structure that each of these countries maintains to combat wildlife trafficking and must be strictly monitored to avoid legitimate industries from masking illegal activity. Furthermore, it should be a target area for law enforcement in that it is necessary for regulatory agencies to have good relations with traders to develop intelligence networks (Halstead, 1994).

Traditional medicines are also smuggled to each of the three countries. Presumably, this is related to the illegal imports coming from China and Hong Kong. The three countries have diaspora populations from China and other parts of Asia and this may account for the demand for traditional medicines. This may warrant further outreach activities as discussed in the Australian section where law enforcement runs campaigns with partners in these communities in an attempt to reduce demand for these illegal products. Each of the countries also has smuggling of plants, particularly orchids, and marine wildlife such as giant clams and coral. Plants and marine wildlife rarely receive attention and may be regulated in a different manner. Coral, for instance, is not a species that Customs would necessarily target. It could be argued that a majority of the research conducted around the illegal trade in wildlife has focused on terrestrial non-human animals. The data fin this study, however, indicates the need to research the trafficking of marine wildlife as well as plants as they clearly feature in this black market. As has been observed in cases of trafficking of terrestrial non-human animals, smuggling of marine wildlife and plants is also most likely resulting in damage to the ecosystems from which they are trafficked. This has not been documented in the literature. This indicates that the three countries should address the smuggling of these species in particular as the amount is significant and it has similar negative environmental consequences as the trafficking of terrestrial wildlife.

Part of this study and of the larger TEC Project is to analyse the presence of networks understood here as 'actors … linked to each other through stable formal or informal relationships of communication and exchange' (Sangiovanni, 2005). Whereas there are a few examples of serious organised crime engaged in wildlife trafficking as detailed above, these are the exception rather than the rule. It is evident from prosecutions and other studies that wildlife trafficking taking place in and out of Australia, New

Zealand, and the UK tend to be individual offenders. They are most likely part of networks that communicate regarding the demand for wildlife in various places, but a vast majority of the time these are informal relationships and networks. They may, in fact, be stable networks, but more research into the offenders needs to be undertaken to determine their stability and resilience.

The main area of difference in this study is the regulation and penalties that each of the countries employs. All are signatories to CITES and their Category 1 status indicates that they have implemented the required legislation to comply with the CITES provisions. Australia has gone a step further; it requires permits for CITES Appendix II imports (and reports noticeably lower levels of illegal imports). It is recommended that New Zealand and the UK consider requiring import permits for CITES Appendix II species as this seems to correlate to Australia's success in this aspect of combating wildlife trafficking. New Zealand and the UK should also make more of an effort to address wildlife trafficking in their territories. In the case of New Zealand, this would mean encouraging the Cook Islands and Niue to join CITES, and in the case of the UK this would mean ensuring that each of the territories has the minimum required legislation. Additionally, they may provide gaps in enforcement that enable traffickers to smuggle illegal wildlife into the UK though more research needs to take place to verify this possibility.

Even before CITES, Australia had banned the export of native wildlife. New Zealand and the UK still allow export of native species within their respective regulatory frameworks. Yet, illegal exports are higher in Australia than in the UK or New Zealand. It is impossible to determine if they would be even higher were there no ban or if the amount of exports is more a reflection of the high amount of biodiversity in Australia, which increases prices and therefore incentive to smuggle. This discussion does not reflect other responses to wildlife trafficking besides the legislation that complies with CITES. For instance, Horne (2013a) indicates that in the Pacific and Oceania, policy response to wildlife trafficking is mostly through other contexts such as biodiversity conservation, environmental sustainability, economic development, or transnational organised crime initiatives. These then undoubtedly affect the amount of wildlife trafficking that is taking place. Furthermore, this research does not capture the multi-lateral agreements or multi-partner initiatives that are taking place particularly those like the Australasian Environmental Law Enforcement and Regulators Network (AELERT) in Oceania or Partnership for Action against Wildlife Crime (PAWS) in the UK.

The penalties that each of these countries imposes might also impact upon the amount of wildlife trafficking that is detected. Australia has very high penalties with fines of up to A$110,000 for individuals and A$550,000 for corporations. Prison sentences can be up to ten years. New Zealand's are slightly less with fines being NZ$100,000 (A$88,000) for individuals and NZ$200,000 (A$176,000) for corporations. The prison sentences are a maximum of five years. The UK's are the least with fines of £5,000 (A$8,550) and no increased penalties for corporations. Technically, fines could be unlimited if the case were tried in the higher court, but this does not happen. The punishments vary wildly, but what is common is that maximum fines and sentences are not given, so punishment for wildlife trafficking in each country is considered weak and not seen as a deterrent to potential wildlife offenders.

Conclusion

Even with the similarities of demographics and geography (island nations), the three countries that were part of this comparative research experience different levels of wildlife trafficking. This is at least the picture given from the number of illegal incidents that are reported to CITES each year. In using this dataset, it is acknowledged that this does not take into account the intra-state internal trafficking that may be happening. And as with all criminological studies, it is based upon reported crimes, so the dark figure of all the incidents of wildlife trafficking that were not discovered is unknown. This may indeed mean that levels of wildlife trafficking within these three nations differ from the data presented here. That being said, the CITES data still provides useful information to guide further studies. In particular, smuggling of plants and marine wildlife warrant more attention in terms of research and law enforcement initiatives as they are prominent within this black market, but have yet to be the focus of prevention efforts.

Variations in the amount of wildlife smuggled in and out of Australia, New Zealand, and the UK cannot be directly correlated to the different regulations or punishments, but a key difference that may be linked to low incidents of illegal imports in Australia is that they require a CITES import permit for Appendix II species. This is stricter than the CITES requirement and is recommended for New Zealand and the UK. Australia has higher punishments for wildlife trafficking and this too may contribute to their comparatively low number of incidents. All countries should revisit how these offenders are punished as the sentences and fines imposed seem nearly always to be at the lowest end of the scale.

Variations in wildlife trafficking incidents do not correlate to the species themselves, since there is a significant amount of overlap in the species trafficked, which indicates similar demand markets (Wyatt, 2012). The differing levels of wildlife trafficking could also stem from another source not detailed here, possibly law enforcement tactics and response, or a social or cultural explanation. Further studies will need to be done in order to determine more fully the cause of the relative success of Australia in combating the illegal wildlife trade. The UK and New Zealand may be able to learn valuable lessons from this kind of further exploration. Other comparative studies on wildlife trafficking (and other green crimes) between nations may prove key in uncovering tactics that can help improve existing policies and prevention strategies. Cooperation and sharing of best practice is essential in order to reduce global networked crime such as the illegal trade in wildlife, which is threatening the unique and irreplaceable species and environments of the world.

References

Alacs, E. and Georges, A. (2008). Wildlife across our borders: A review of the illegal trade in Australia. *Australian Journal of Forensic Sciences*, 40(2): 147-60.

Altherr, S. and Freyer, D. (2001). *Morbidity and mortality in private husbandry of reptiles*. Report by Pro Wildlife to the Royal Society for the Prevention of Cruelty to Animals, Horsham: RSPCA.

Australian Customs (2010). *Annual Report 2009-2010*. Canberra: Australian Customs and Border Protection Service, October.

Blindell, J. (2006). 21st century policing: The role of the police in the detection, investigation and prosecution of environmental crime, *ACPR Issues*, 2: 1-8.

Bricknell, S. (2010). *Environmental crime in Australia*. Research and Public Policy Series No. 109, Canberra: Australian Institute of Criminology.

Carpenter, A.I., Robson, R.O., Rowcliffe, M.J. and Watkinson, A.R. (2004). The impacts of international and national governance changes on a traded resource: A case study of Madagascar and its chameleon trade. *Biological Conservation*, 123: 279-287.

COTES (2005). *The control of trade in endangered species (enforcement) (amendment) regulations*. Retrieved from www.legislation.gov.uk/uksi/2005/1674/resources

CITES (2012). *National Laws for Implementation of the Convention, Notification to the Parties No. 2012/036*. Geneva, 18 April.

DSEWPaC (2010). *Biennial report submitted pursuant to resolution Conf. 11.17 (Rev. CoP14) on national reports*. Department of Sustainability, Environment, Water, Population and Communities.

Elliott, L. (2011).*Transnational environmental crime: Applying network theory to an investigation of illegal trade, criminal activity and law enforcement responses*. Transnational Environmental Crime Project Working Paper 1/2011, Canberra: Department of International Relations, Australian National University.

Fisher, M.C., and Garner, T.W.J. (2007). The relationship between the emergence of Batrachochytrium dendrobatidis, the international trade in amphibians and introduced amphibian species. *Fungal Biology Reviews*, 21(1): 2-9.

Halstead, B. (1994).*Wildlife legislation in Australia: Trafficking provisions*. Canberra: Australian Institute of Criminology.

Holden, J. (ed.) (1997). *Trade in CITES-listed birds to and from New Zealand*. Sydney: TRAFFIC Oceania.

Horne, D. (2013a). *Policy responses to transnational wildlife crime in the Asia-Pacific – part 1: Global and regional policy context and a potential framework for optimal national policy*. Transnational Environmental Crime Project Working Paper 1/2013, Canberra: Department of International Relations, Australian National University.

Horne, D. (2013b). *Policy responses to transnational wildlife crime in the Asia-Pacific – part 2: Policy responses at the national level and preliminary gap analysis*. Transnational Environmental Crime Project Working Paper 2/2013, Canberra: Department of International Relations, Australian National University.

IFAW (International Fund for Animal Welfare) (2008). *Killing with keystrokes: An investigation of the illegal wildlife trade on the world wide web*. Retrieved from www.ifaw.org/sites/default/files/Killing%20with%20Keystrokes.pdf.

Lowther, J., Cook, D., and Roberts, M. (2002). *Crime and punishment in the wildlife trade*. Godalming: WWF/TRAFFIC, Retrieved from www.wwf.org.uk/filelibrary/pdf/crime and punishment.pdf.

New Zealand Government (2010). *Organised crime in New Zealand*. Retrieved from www.ofcanz.govt.nz/sites/default/files/Organised-Crime-in-NZ-2010-Public-Version.pdf.

Putt, J., and Anderson, K. (2007). *A national study of crime in the Australian fishing industry*. Research and Public Policy Series No. 76, Canberra: Australian Institute for Criminology.

Rosen, G., and Smith, K. (2010). Summarizing the evidence on the international trade in illegal wildlife. *Eco Health*, 7: 24-32.

Sangiovanni, M.E. (2005). Transnational networks and security threats. *Cambridge Review of International Affairs*, 18(1): 7-13.

Schneider, J. (2012). *Sold into extinction: The global trade in endangered species*. Santa Barbara, CA: Praeger.

Tapley, B., Griffiths, R., and Bride, I. (2011). Dynamics of the trade in reptiles and amphibians within the United Kingdom over a ten-year period. *Herpetological Journal*, 21: 27-34.

TIES (1989). *Trade in endangered species Act*. Retrieved from www. legislation. govt. nz/act/public/1989/0018/latest/whole.html

TRAFFIC (2011). *TRAFFIC bulletin seizures and prosecutions: March 1997-April 2011*. Cambridge: TRAFFIC International.

Wyatt, T. (2012). Uncovering the significance of and motivation for wildlife trafficking. In Brisman, A. and South, N. (Eds.), *Routledge international handbook of green criminology*. London: Routledge.

Wyatt, T. (2013). The local context of wildlife trafficking: The Heathrow animal reception centre. In Westerhuis, D., Walters, R. and Wyatt, T. (Eds.), *Emerging issues in green criminology: Exploring power, justice and harm*. Basingstoke: Palgrave Macmillan.

4

Role of NGOs in Countering Wildlife Trafficking

Angus Nurse, Middlesex University, UK

Introduction

Illegal trafficking in wildlife represents a significant problem in the area of wildlife crime. Schneider (2008) and others have identified that wildlife trafficking has pushed some species to the brink of extinction and remains a threat to others. Nelleman et al. (2014) estimate an unsustainable number of between 20,000 and 25,000 African elephants are killed each year by poachers. Wyatt (2013) identifies that while there is undoubtedly a large 'dark figure' of unknown criminal activity, the estimate of illegal wildlife trade accepted by most experts is between USD 10 and USD 20 billion annually, not including fisheries or timber.

Wildlife trafficking is now accepted as a major area of criminality attracting the attention of law enforcement policymakers and scholars (Wyatt, 2013; Nurse, 2015). Within environmental law discourse, wildlife protection laws are an area of considerable activity both internationally and within domestic policy (Nurse, 2015). International law frameworks such as the Convention on International Trade in Endangered Species of Wild Fauna and Flora (CITES) and associated laws such as the European Union (EU) Wildlife Trade Regulations aim to combat illegal exploitation of wildlife and provide for sanctions against offenders committing wildlife trafficking offences. Yet despite growing environmental awareness among law enforcement, the efforts of a variety of Non-Governmental Organizations (NGOs) to influence the wildlife protection policy agenda and periodic improvements in legislative frameworks, wildlife laws remain outside the remit of mainstream criminal justice. Their enforcement is often a fringe area of policing whose public policy and enforcement response significantly relies on NGOs.

Nurse (2012) identified that it is in enforcement rather than the legislative framework that problems in wildlife protection mostly occur. Wildlife crime policing primarily adopts reactive apprehension, detection and punishment paradigms rather than proactive preventative ones (Wellsmith, 2011; Nurse, 2012, 2015). This article argues that due to failures in traditional criminal justice responses, the global wildlife enforcement movement made up of international and transnational organizations like WWF (World Wildlife Fund) and Humane Society International and complemented with policy networks such as Animal Defenders International and the Coalition against Wildlife Trafficking (CAWT) provides a model for transnational law enforcement. White's (2012) regulation theory analysis identifies that third parties such as NGOs often play a significant role in investigating and exposing environmental harm and offending and have become a necessity for effective environmental law enforcement. In wildlife trafficking, NGOs are an essential part not only of practical enforcement regimes, but also the development of effective policy acting as: policy advisors, researchers, field investigators, expert witnesses at court, scientific advisors, casework managers, and, in the case of a small number of organizations, prosecutors playing a significant evidence-based role in policy development and law enforcement (Nurse, 2013a).

Critically examining NGOs anti-wildlife trafficking practices, this article argues that while over-reliance on NGOs may be undesirable they have become effective enforcement/policy actors stepping in to address the failure of states and national justice systems to deal with this area of transnational environmental crime.

Contextualizing Wildlife Trafficking

Wildlife trafficking makes up a significant category of wildlife crime (in both volume and economic value) and is a specific offense type incorporating a range of offences including taking, illegal transport, possession, fraud, illegal sale and cruelty (Wyatt, 2013; Nurse, 2013b). Interpol's (2014) definition of wildlife crime as 'the illegal exploitation of the world's wild flora and fauna' is primarily based around wildlife crime conceptualized as wildlife trafficking; illegal exploitation and trade. Green criminology often classifies wildlife crime according to White's (2008a) notion of animal rights and species justice, which deals with animal abuse and suffering (including crimes impacting on animals in the wild or at least living predominantly away from urban conurbations) and cruelty or welfare offences involving farmed animals. Wildlife crime may also be classified according to broader conceptions of environmental or ecological crimes, considering environmental justice in relation to the use of natural resources in defined geographical areas (White, 2008b). A number of scholars have explored wildlife trafficking as a growing area of transnational crime; prominent within the hierarchy of global crimes (Zimmerman 2003; Schneider, 2008; South and Wyatt, 2011; Wyatt, 2009, 2013). Wildlife trafficking can thus be interpreted and classified as part of a green perspective (South, 1998), which considers crimes that affect the environment and biodiversity as requiring a criminal justice response that reflects environmental, ecological justice, or species rights concerns, and an increased public sensitivity to crimes causing environmental harm. In accordance with notions of species justice, wildlife trafficking can include animal abuse offences consisting of 'socially unacceptable behavior that intentionally causes unnecessary pain, suffering, or distress to and/or death of an animal (Ascione, 1993) particularly given the intentional disruption in the lives of animals that exist in a wild state (Nurse, 2011). Synergy exists between wildlife trade's similarity with classical positivist notions of crime (Vold and Bernard, 1986) and offenders clearly motivated by profit (particularly with respect to trade in endangered species which can sell for thousands of pounds) and involved in other forms of crime (Hutton, 1998; Linzey, 2009). Schneider (2008) and Lowther et al. (2002) found that organized crime recognizes wildlife crime as a 'soft option' where its traditional operations and transit routes can be utilized with a lesser risk of enforcement activity. Thus, wildlife trafficking can often be contextualized as rational, profit-driven crime where wildlife represents a resource to be exploited. Anthropocentric notions of wildlife as an exploitable resource arguably dominate at least some aspects of criminality involved in wildlife trafficking. This is especially the case in the supply and retail end where commercial considerations dictate the manner in which wildlife is acquired and sold.

Policing Wildlife Trafficking

The majority of policing theory and literature is based on a model of social organization which sees crime as primarily dealt with through community engagement and a combination of proactive and reactive policing (Newburn, 2008; Joyce, 2010). However, wildlife trafficking, consisting of initial poaching incidents, subsequent transit and arguably illegal sale offences presents specific policing challenges; not just for rural policing and game agencies frequently lacking in both the expertise and resources necessary to deal with non-standard policing challenges, i.e. matters that officers do not routinely encounter and may not be trained to deal with (Kirkwood, 1994; Nurse, 2012) but also for policy development. The effects of geography alone can have significant impacts on policing wildlife trafficking by negatively influencing the availability of resources, response times and the speed with which support services can be provided (Mawby and Yarwood, 2010). In addition, the transnational nature of wildlife trafficking, crossing jurisdictions and requiring the collaboration of a range of different enforcement officers potentially frustrates effective enforcement action given the territorial nature of policing operations and jurisdiction-specific legislation. Wyatt (2013) identifies that the transnational nature of wildlife trafficking requires a coordinated approach across borders. Accordingly, several agencies may be involved in enforcement including customs, border and immigration agencies, police, environmental protection agencies and conservation monitoring agencies. Thus NGOs, identified by White (2012) as integral to environmental enforcement according to regulation theory, which dictates that environmental enforcement cannot be carried out by statutory policing agencies alone, become increasingly important in wildlife crime enforcement (Nurse, 2015) given their ability to operate internationally. Roberts et al. (2001) identified that enforcers and regulators working in the area of wildlife crime 'often lack resources and expertise' while Nurse (2012) and Wellsmith (2011) both identified a continued lack of resources as endemic to continued enforcement and policy failure in the wildlife crime arena.

Anti-wildlife trafficking legislation is arguably also a weakness where legislation does not entirely ban wildlife trade, but instead seeks to regulate it, creating an environment where the legal and illegal trades coexist (Zimmerman, 2003; Wyatt, 2013; Nurse, 2015). Sollund (2013), for example, argues that 'CITES can be criticized for legitimating trade and trafficking in animals and for prolonging and encouraging abuse and species decline by regarding nonhuman species as exploitable resources'. Wildlife protection laws are mainly reactive, creating offences that are punished after the fact rather than containing preventative measures; they generally allow for the continued exploitation of wildlife subject to certain controls. Wildlife trafficking is primarily economically driven; wildlife is a resource from which individuals gain profit and demand for wildlife or wildlife products (including parts or derivatives) ensures that such markets continue to exist. Economic incentives for wildlife exploitation operate at individual, group (e.g. corporate or organization) and state level where income derived from wildlife can provide individual benefit in the form of direct profit

(Nurse, 2011, 2012; South and Wyatt, 2011) or contribute significantly to a state's economy e.g. through wildlife tourism or sanctioned hunting (Brockington et al., 2008). Accordingly wildlife trafficking can theoretically be reduced where offenders are persuaded to desist from offending by intensifying their fear of punishment and increasing their costs. Thus punishment can be limited to actions considered necessary to prevent offenders from 'choosing' to commit such wildlife crime (Clarke and Cornish, 2001; Piquero and Tibbetts, 2002). Stallworthy (2008) argues that 'traditional market based perspectives are broadly accepting of legal regulation as a constraint on wealth generating activities; where restricted to the correction of market imperfections'. Wyatt (2013) identifies that laws to curb destruction of wildlife have been in existence for hundreds of years, and laws explicitly regulating the trade in wildlife have been developed fairly consistently throughout the 20th century. Yet the effectiveness and development of wildlife laws and their associated enforcement has undergone significant change from the late 20th century onwards as greater knowledge of threats to wildlife and the expansion of globalised markets have required increased wildlife protection (Ehrenfeld, 2003). However, questions remain over the effectiveness of a response solely driven by criminal justice agencies and which fails to incorporate civil society organizations.

Failures in Traditional Criminal Justice Responses

The reality of current policy across jurisdictions is that it broadly treats all wildlife offenders as rational (financially motivated) criminals subject to deterrence principles via a suitably punitive regime (Nurse, 2015; 2011). While there is some recognition that illegal wildlife trade continues 'due to complex socioeconomic and political conditions that are often beyond the scope of targeted international programs and agreements' (Wyler and Sheikh, 2013) enforcement action is primarily targeted at the supply rather than demand side of wildlife trafficking. Such enforcement action is primarily reactive, notwithstanding the existence of some preventative methods such as rhino dehorning (Biggs et al., 2013) and is overwhelmingly punitive. Yet, the primary motivators identified for different offender types which determine that offenders involved in wildlife trafficking have various motivations (Nurse, 2011; Wyatt, 2013) indicates that different elements drive each offender type making a uniform approach to offending and enforcement ineffectual. The wildlife trafficking enforcement regime thus requires modification, allowing for action appropriate to the circumstances of the offender and specific nature of the offence to be taken and which distinguishes between different elements within wildlife trafficking such as killing of wildlife for parts or derivatives, trapping, transit, retail and even purchasing offences. Current sanctions policy is primarily based around a more punitive approach and sanctions aimed at negating any benefit offenders derive from their activity. But an argument can be made that increased sentencing and use of prison has been unsuccessful in mainstream criminal justice (Wilson, 1985) and so the evidence that it will be effective in reducing or preventing wildlife crime is lacking, particularly in respect of those offenders such as terror groups and militias for whom such punitive sanctions and the threat of incarceration are likely accepted and even tolerated risks. This is not to suggest lack of confidence in the criminal justice system as a tool for dealing with wildlife trafficking, but indicates a need to consider the specific nature of offending and to incorporate preventative and harm reduction measures which consider the realities of wildlife trafficking and its associated criminality. Rather than solely apprehending offenders after offences have been committed and biodiversity loss achieved, greater efforts should be made to attempt situational crime prevention. This means making the physical cost of committing the crime prohibitive as well as increasing the actual cost and removing the perception that wildlife crime may be seen as a 'soft' option (Wellsmith, 2011). This is an area where conservation NGOs, active on the ground and engaging with local communities are able to bring enforcement benefits (discussed later in this paper).

Considerable research evidence indicates that existing wildlife law regimes do not work in their implementation rather than in their basic legislative provisions. Practical enforcement problems endemic to the UK's wildlife law system were identified by Nurse (2003, 2009, 2011 and 2012) and Wellsmith (2010, 2011). Their respective analyses identified a system consisting of legislation inadequate to the task of wildlife protection, subject to an equally inconsistent enforcement regime (albeit one where individual police officers and NGOs contribute significant amounts of time and effort within their own area) and one that fails to address the specific nature of wildlife offending. Similar problems have been reported in the US context (President's Advisory Council on Wildlife Trafficking, 2014) albeit in the form of the US Fish and Wildlife Service, the US has the statutory (federal) wildlife enforcement agency that has previously been identified as desirable when analyzing deficiencies in other jurisdictions (Cook et al., 2002). White (2012) identifies that third parties such as NGOs often play a significant role in investigating and exposing environmental harm and offending and have become a necessity for effective environmental law enforcement. In most jurisdictions, wildlife law is effectively a fringe area of policing whose public policy response is significantly influenced by NGOs (Nurse, 2012) and which continues to rely on NGOs as an integral part of the enforcement regime. Conceptually four basic enforcement models for wildlife crime policing exist as follows (Nurse, 2015):

- Enforcement by mainstream statutory police agency (including customs authority)
- Enforcement by specialist environmental regulatory agency (state environmental protection agencies, Fish & Wildlife Service)
- Enforcement by conservation, natural resource, parks agency
- Enforcement by NGO

NGOs are an essential part not only of practical wildlife enforcement regimes, but also the development of effective policy (Nurse, 2013a). NGOs are often the means through which human rights abuses and other failures to comply with international law norms come to light. Marcinkutë (2011) argues that in non-western countries, especially authoritarian regimes with relatively low social-economic developments, weak civil society and a lack of democracy human rights NGOs are seen as the threat to state sovereignty and state's authority'. Similarly, wildlife protection and conservation NGOs exert considerable pressure through campaigning, policy development or active enforcement. NGOs operating in the field of wildlife crime develop their policies from the ideological positions of: *(a) Moral culpability*: censuring activities that they believe are morally wrong; *(b)Political priorities* : censuring activities that they consider should be given a higher profile in public policy (which may include issues that they consider are worthy of being a higher law enforcement priority or which should be the subject of law enforcement activity and/or legislative change); and *(c)Animal Rights* : a belief in rights for animals which includes policies that demonstrate either the case for animal rights or which demonstrate breaches of the existing rights which animals are said to have (Nurse, 2013a).

Within wildlife trafficking discourse NGOs are able to monitor the actions and effectiveness of environmental enforcers and regulators and provide support and alternative enforcement and policy strategies where statutory regulators are seen as ineffective. For example, in principle, specialist environmental agencies such as the US Fish and Wildlife Service (USFWS), the Environmental Protection Agency (US) and English Nature and the Environment Agency (UK) can provide both regulatory and criminal enforcement options in environmental crime. However, limitations are often placed on these agencies by virtue of the legislation which gives them their powers, and their tightly defined jurisdiction (Stallworthy, 2008). In practice; legislative and jurisdictional restrictions may dictate that such bodies carry our enforcement activities in a particular way. The same is true of enforcement by parks and conservation bodies who operate within the confines of a jurisdictional brief which usually limits their activities to their specific environmental or conservation remit. However, Patten et al. (2014) identify that game wardens, for example, are subject to both environmental and human caused dangers in the line of duty. Conservation and game wardens are employed in high conflict areas (Eliason, 2006) where personal threats are an integral part of their duties, particularly in game areas where militarized poaching has become an emergent threat. The reality is that the pace, level of sophistication and globalized nature of wildlife and forest crime is beyond the capacity of many countries and individual organizations to address. Transnational organized crime's involvement in illegal trafficking of wildlife is now recognized as fact (Nelleman et al., 2014) yet the resources provided to game wardens and conservation agents to deal with organized crime are often lacking. While Nelleman et al. (2014) identify that over 1,000 Tanzanian rangers have recently received specialized training covering 'tracking of poachers, tactics and wildlife crime scene management' such resources and training are not consistently supplied or utilized effectively by all jurisdictions. This risks the possibility of displacement as poachers and traffickers identify those areas vulnerable to poaching or where enforcement is carried out by ill-equipped conservation workers in lieu of professional police. However, Patten et al. (2014) identify that, at least in the United States, game wardens are also required to deal with 'mainstream' crimes of violence and regularly encounter a clientele armed with handguns, knives, shotguns and rifles thus training in a range of law enforcement and aggression diffusion techniques is required. Traditional avenues of support for peace officers may also be unavailable or some distance away due to the remote nature of game reserves, national parks and other countryside areas. In addition, Ayling (2013) identifies that wildlife poaching 'can be at least tacitly supported by poor communities because the financial benefits to the community outweigh those available from legitimate employment or state welfare services'. Ayling (2013) also identifies resilience and adaptation as being key aspects of organized crime groups' success in wildlife trafficking. South and Wyatt's (2011) analysis identifies the complexity of organized crime involved in the illegal wildlife trade consistent with the findings of other researchers who have identified adaptation of organized crime groups to wildlife trafficking (Elliott, 2009; Nurse, 2012, 2013). However, for 'terror groups' and militias, recognizing the ready availability of protected fauna and flora as a revenue stream and adapting operating practices to exploit this is not unusual. Ayling discusses the resilience of such groups such that the rigid hierarchical structures of other organized crime groups need not apply (Glenny, 2008) and 'opposition from authorities and changes in the economic and social conditions in which they operate' can be adapted to (Ayling, 2013). Accordingly illicit wildlife trafficking becomes a persistent and ongoing activity and not only will trafficking methods adapt to accommodate new enforcement efforts but personnel will also adapt or be replaced as required to secure the longevity of the business. Accordingly, new approaches to dealing with contemporary organized crime involvement in transnational wildlife crime and wildlife trafficking will need to be developed that recognize the varied behavior and motivations for offending (Eliason, 2003; South and Wyatt, 2011; Nurse, 2011, 2013). Homogeneous categorization of wildlife trafficking crime risks the development of law and public policy inadequate to the task of reducing wildlife trafficking and dealing with new forms of wildlife criminality such as militarized poaching. The traditional approach to offending, which inevitably resorts to a detection apprehension and punishment approach is unsuited to the complexity of wildlife trafficking criminality and may be ineffective as wildlife trafficking evolves and new forms and categorizations of offender develop. Across jurisdictions, a range of problems have been identified within wildlife law enforcement as follows:

- Lack of resources
- Inconsistency of legislation
- Inconsistency in sentencing
- Lack of police priority and inconsistency in policing approaches

Wyler and Sheikh (2013) argue that lax law enforcement and inadequate wildlife security measures are a factor in levels of wildlife crime and that 'even where heightened security measures to protect wildlife are implemented, they have not consistently had a deterrent effect'. Indeed there is evidence that within wildlife trafficking, offenders employ increasingly sophisticated and elaborate mechanisms which law enforcement fails to keep pace with (Nelleman et al., 2014). An April 2013 Resolution of the UN Commission on Crime, Prevention and Criminal Justice (endorsed by the UN Economic and Social Council in July 2013) encourages UN member states to 'make illicit trafficking in wild fauna and flora a serious crime when organized criminal groups are involved', effectively placing it on the same level as human trafficking and drug trafficking. Wildlife trafficking should, therefore now be placed in most jurisdictions definition of serious crime and be prosecuted and sentenced accordingly. However, the reality of wildlife crime enforcement is that inconsistency and a lack of proper training and prosecutorial and sentencing guidance hampers the efficiency of court proceedings in some jurisdictions. Some NGOs have argued that existing sentencing options could be better used as wildlife crime offences rarely attract penalties at the upper end of the available scale with fines tending to be at the lower or middle end. Prison sentences are also used ineffectively or not at all in the case of corporate offenders (Akella and Allan, 2012; Nurse, 2012). Lowther, Cook and Roberts (2002) writing on the wildlife trade for WWF and TRAFFIC argued that the imposition of low penalties was a feature in the majority of prosecuted cases.

NGO Perspectives

NGOs are not usually involved in practical law enforcement, but are significantly involved in wildlife crime where various NGOs assist the police and prosecutors actively in detecting, investigating and prosecuting crime. NGOs have traditionally collated information on the amount of wildlife crime that exists while the statutory enforcement authorities (police, Customs etc.) have only recorded crime data on an ad-hoc basis (Conway, 1999; Nurse, 2008). One consequence of this is that NGOs have, traditionally, better understood wildlife crime levels, policing and criminal behavior problems and the reality of how incidents such as wildlife trafficking impact on local communities. This gives NGOs considerable influence in directing the law enforcement agenda to their areas of specific interest and areas in which they have acquired considerable expertise. In effect, wildlife crime allows for the study of 'private policing' in an area of criminal justice policy where a considerable amount of law enforcement activity is still carried out on a voluntary basis by private bodies. The UK, for example, has the RSPCA's uniformed Inspectorate (in respect of animal welfare crimes and wildlife cruelty crimes such as badger baiting and badger digging) and the organization retains its role as prosecuting agency. The RSPB's Investigations Section also takes the lead on the investigation of some wildlife crime cases (those affecting wild birds) before they are taken over by the public prosecutor the Crown Prosecution Service (CPS). The League against Cruel Sports has also taken a lead on monitoring the effectiveness of the Hunting Act 2004, providing assistance and advice to the police and taking prosecutions to ensure the law is being used. TRAFFIC is arguably the main collator and monitor of illegal wildlife trade and trafficking, operating internationally through its various offices in a way that policing agencies are broadly unable to achieve (albeit Interpol provides for information exchange and intelligence support to national police forces). Thus whereas in some areas, such as street crime, police functions are being privatized with the introduction of private security patrols, police community support officers (PCSOs) and street wardens (Fielding and Innes, 2006), wildlife crime is an area where the policing function has traditionally been carried out by NGOs where it involves non-standard offences. Arguably it is only recently that the police have become active in operational law enforcement of wildlife and environmental offences remaining under pressure from NGOs to become more involved. Given the lack of centralized expertise in wildlife crime police and prosecutors in a range of jurisdictions still rely heavily on NGOs. Thus US citizens have come to understand and expect that NGOs like the Sierra Club, Defenders of Wildlife and Earth justice will take action where federal government agencies fail to do so. This picture is replicated in other countries.

However, the role of NGOs as enforcers or campaigners varies according to the types of crime involved, with different policy perspectives pursued in respect of game offences and poaching, habitat destruction and pollution of rural environments, or offences involving domestic/farm animals and animal welfare and cruelty offences. The relationship between NGOs and policymakers also varies so that, for example, game offences are considered to be effectively policed within the UK's strong game and anti-poaching legislation, with good co-operation between police and game rearing staff over poaching, but the same is not true of wildlife offences. Game rearing staff regularly report poaching offences (which directly affect their livelihoods and the rural economy) to statutory agencies. But they may be reluctant to have the same involvement in wildlife offences such as bird of prey prosecution where game rearing staff are often suspects and may be in conflict with the police and conservationists over the appropriateness and legitimacy of enforcement action and rural crime policy.

Complex attitudes to wildlife crime exist within rural communities where resistance to legislation to control or criminalize traditional rural field sports or to limit wildlife use and exploitation continues, while NGOs sometimes pursue an abolitionist agenda on moral grounds seeking to criminalize or regulate rural activities such as shooting and fishing. The campaign against the UKs Hunting Act 2004 was often characterized as 'town versus country' (Burns et al., 2000), similarly the imposition of western environmentalist perspectives on rural communities that depend on income from wildlife risks perpetuating perceptions that affluent sections of society seek to impose their will on poorer rural members of society and pursue an idealized notion of rurality. There is, however, arguably a three way divide between the rural poor actively involved in rural pursuits, the gentrified rich who are involved in both a managerial and participatory capacity, and the new urban/cosmopolitan middle classes who seek to influence the classes above and below them. Lowe and Ginsberg (2002) concluded that the US animal rights movement has a disproportionately well-educated membership reflecting what Parkin (1968) called 'middle class radicalism'. Certainly the major UK wildlife crime NGOs, while not all pursuing policies from an animal rights perspective, represent a professional movement comprising large professional organizations (comparable with medium to large businesses) rather than being a grass roots or 'activists' movement. Figures for certain major wildlife or animal protection NGOs show annual running costs typically in excess of £50 million per organization (see for example RSPB, 2010; RSPCA, 2007). The organizations' considerable public support (the RSPB has over a million members), together with the resources available for campaigning and political lobbying, allows the main environmental NGOs to take the lead in promoting rural and wildlife crime as important issues. It also places the organizations in a position to employ expertise, for example specialist investigators and political lobbyists, promoting their policy objectives and adopting a dominant policy or scientific position, while their socio-economic position allows them to exploit that perceived expertise and dominate the policy debate on rural crime.

NGOs Ideology and Social Change

Beyond addressing statutory enforcement and policy failures or a perceived lack of attention to an issue, NGOs also act as agents of social change. NGOs primarily achieve their objectives through public campaigning to raise awareness of an issue, commonly commissioning or carrying out their own research to prove their issue-based case, to lobby for legislative change or manipulate public opinion on policy priorities or the need for government intervention. NGOs like the American Society for the Prevention of Cruelty to Animals (ASPCA), Royal Society for the Protection of Birds (RSPB), Royal Society for the Prevention of Cruelty to Animals (RSPCA), Defenders of Wildlife, Humane Society, League Against Cruel Sports (LACS), and World Wildlife Fund (WWF) expend considerable publicity resources to ensure that the public is aware that environmental crime and specific wildlife crime issues are major priorities. So too, have more broadly environment-based NGOs like the Sierra Club and Earth justice. Glossy reports, press releases, direct mail campaigns, newspaper, television and radio advertisements, newspaper feature stories and extensive (often innovative) use of social media and viral marketing all contribute to the public's knowledge of NGO involvement in environmental crime and understanding of contemporary policy perspectives. Thus, unsurprisingly, UK members of the public wishing to report wildlife offences routinely telephone the RSPB, RSPCA, LACS et al. rather than mainstream policing agencies. This reflects both the perception that members of the public have that these are crimes that the police may not investigate and also illustrates the success of NGOs in promoting their involvement in wildlife crime investigation and their policy development. Such reporting, however, distorts the picture of wildlife crime somewhat as NGO publication of wildlife crime figures is naturally tailored to suit ideological, campaigning and policy needs. Thus reporting may reflect a species specific conservationist message (e.g. number of wolves, birds, etc. illegally killed or trafficked) a broad campaigning message (worsening levels of crime or inadequacies of legislation) or an ideological position (moral wrong of animal harm, demonization of hunters or other deviant groups) commensurate with the NGOs ideological stance as campaigning, policing or lobbying organization (Nurse, 2013a). Arguably it is generally in the interests of individual NGOs to produce figures that show a worsening picture of environmental crime given that many NGOs are also charitable organizations reliant on voluntary public donations in order to achieve environmental protection priorities.

Nurse (2013a) has identified that at one end of the spectrum there are large NGOs existing as 'conservation corporations' achieving legitimacy within social structures such that they are seen as part of the establishment. Such organizations gain legitimacy through Royal charters in the UK (e.g. the RSPB, RSPCA) in a manner that risks their being viewed by other NGOs as illegitimate by virtue of being part of a failed establishment system which more activist NGOs and environmentalists consider should not be engaged with. Other NGOs might gain legitimacy by consistent engagement with policy discourse or active law enforcement activity. Jasper (1997) in discussing 'post-material' social movements explained that mainstream environmental organizations are comprised mainly of people already integrated into their society's political, economic and educational systems and who by virtue of their affluence did not need to campaign for basic rights for themselves but could pursue protections and benefits for others. Major environmental NGOs illustrate this perspective, having grown from their activist roots to embrace animal protection and conservation corporations with considerable economic and political power (Nurse, 2013a).

White (2012) applies contemporary regulation theory to environmental crime, recognizing the poor level of resources, meagre budgets and low staffing levels that exist in environmental law enforcement given the size and scale of environmental problems. Such statutory enforcement failures add to the marginalization of environmental crime and leave a vacuum that has increasingly been filled by NGOs adopting policy development and practical enforcement roles (White, 2012; Nurse, 2013a), with a number of NGOs actively investigating and prosecuting environmental and wildlife crimes. NGO approaches often emphasize the importance of the criminal law and frequently include calls for tougher sentences, more punitive measures for wildlife crime and identify species' survival threats posed by wildlife trafficking (Nurse, 2011, 2012). They also employ a regulatory approach to compliance. Nelleman et al. (2014) identify that in the field of trafficking in wildlife international collaborations exist such as the International Consortium on Combating Wildlife Crime (ICCWC), which includes CITES, UNODC, INTERPOL, the World Bank and WCO. There is also the Coalition against Wildlife Trafficking (CAWT). Such networks, together with increased collaboration amongst agencies, such as with UNEP and with individual countries provides a means through which at international level structured support can be given to countries, in the fields of policing, customs, prosecution and the judiciary. Yet wildlife law enforcement remains predominantly a domestic issue making use of national police, customs or conservation agencies for enforcement.

Martens (2005) identifies that NGOs can have considerable impact as change agents in environmental law beyond the classical role of NGOs as watchdogs over governmental operations, by becoming active participants in the implementation of environmental law. Public policy campaigning is an area where policy networks develop either as loose or structured collections of individuals or groups that work together to influence an area of public policy. Marsh and Rhodes (1992) explain that 'the existence of a policy network both has an influence on, although it clearly does not determine, policy outcomes and reflects the relative status, or even power, of the particular interests in a broad policy area'. In wildlife crime, however, NGOs have gone further by determining policy outcomes and have had a significant role in developing and driving public policy. For example, practical investigative casework by the RSPB highlighted the difficulties of prosecuting offenders for disturbance of protected wild birds at the nest in the UK. Having identified the problem through a number of failed cases, the RSPB successfully campaigned for a change in the wording of the legislation through an amendment to the Wildlife and Countryside Act 1981 which the charity initially 'sponsored' by way of encouraging an MP to pursue a private member's bill. Similarly, the efforts of NGOs like WWF, International Fund for Animal Welfare (IFAW) and the Tiger Trust bring considerable public attention to the threats to endangered species from wildlife trafficking and those NGOs operating practical on the ground enforcement supplement the activities of conservation management agencies.

In most campaigning areas, a formal or structured policy network might be seen to operate with the aim of influencing a change in policy. However, the transnational nature of wildlife trafficking has historically meant that enforcement policies are drawn up by NGOs with either a single issue or a single species perspective (e.g. preventing cruelty, protecting tigers, stopping elephant poaching). However, in respect of wildlife trafficking, the CAWT represents a broad transnational public-private coalition combining government and NGO partners from the UK, US, Chile, India and Australia, including some notable international NGOs. This article has identified that enforcement policy has historically been reactive and focused on supply-side offending. However, the CAWT's mission statement identifies both wildlife law enforcement (reactive) and demand reduction activities (proactive) as its core activities. This means that a single campaign, backed by a number of different organizations can be co-ordinated, providing for both collective and individual action aimed at addressing wildlife trafficking in both its practical and political contexts.

While criminal laws are primarily enforced by public bodies (police, customs, and environmental agencies), Slapper and Kelly (2012) identify that NGOs, representing private interests, can be active in criminal enforcement in various jurisdictions. Some NGOs take a hands-on approach to prosecution and challenging Government enforcement inadequacies, while others view themselves as primarily having an advisory or scientific role. As discussed earlier in this article, some NGOs pursue active engagement in wildlife law enforcement by employing professional investigators; consistent with ideological beliefs that wildlife laws are inconsistently or inadequately enforced by statutory agencies and require dedicated resources (Nurse, 2013b). However, NGOs, unbound by restrictions on state prosecutors are able to pursue cases of international significance and which establish specific points of law or principle in wildlife and environmental protection.

Conclusion

NGOs are an important component of some enforcement activity (e.g. as expert advisers) yet continued NGO enforcement of wildlife and other environmental crimes is arguably undesirable where NGOs adopt the role of lead enforcer. This risks enforcement policy being ideologically driven, reflecting morality-based ideology rather than pure law enforcement perspectives and adherence to the rule that are binding on statutory enforcers. While in principle NGO involvement is necessary when public enforcement falls down, in practice NGOs often lack the resources and practical experience of the full range of policing techniques to fully investigate and prosecute crimes; thus NGO enforcement becomes primarily based on apprehension and punishment rather than incorporating required crime prevention techniques (Wellsmith, 2011; Nurse, 2013a).

However, by providing for a public/private partnership incorporating a range of NGOs and government agencies in various countries, partnerships like ICCWC and CAWT represent a means through which effective action can be taken against wildlife trafficking. Given limited resources and the fact that law enforcement is rarely a priority for NGO resources (Nurse, 2013a) decisions must be made on which enforcement priorities should be pursued by NGOs. This risks enforcement becoming subject to the private interests and campaigning objectives of an NGO and implemented selectively, rather than being conducted in the public interest and in accordance with public policy priorities. White (2012) also notes that some NGOs justify using illegal means to achieve particular aims, particularly where enforcement is allied to an ideological position on law enforcement or rural crime e.g. a fundamental opposition to the lawfulness of game shooting or field sports. This can make effective collaboration between NGOs and official law enforcement agencies problematic (White, 2012) and risk undermining the legitimacy of enforcement action.

NGOs operate their enforcement activities from a particular perspective (Nurse, 2013a) so that some enforcement action may be intended to achieve a campaigning objective, some might be approached from a moral perspective seeking to punish activities that the organization disapproves of, and some might be pursued in order to highlight inadequacies in current law (Nurse, 2013a). Thus wildlife policing might be pursued from an ideological rather than a 'pure' public protection perspective. While this does not imply criticism of any particular NGO, the interests of law and order should be paramount in wildlife policing. Arguably major networks such as ICCWC and CAWT achieve this via approaches geared towards not just reactive enforcement, but also preventative action and development of coordinated policy that takes a holistic approach to wildlife trafficking as both a supply and demand problem. While the involvement of statutory national enforcers may still be required to achieve effective practical enforcement of wildlife trafficking problems, such networks offer hope for a more coordinated approach to global wildlife trafficking problems.

References

Akella, A.S. and Allan, C. (2012). *Dismantling wildlife crime*. Washington: World Wildlife Fund.

Ascione, F.R. (1993). Children who are cruel to animals: A review of research and implications for developmental psychopathology. *Anthrozoos*, 4:226-227.

Ayling, J. (2013). What sustains wildlife crime? Rhino horn trading and the resilience of criminal networks. *Journal of International Wildlife Law & Policy*, 16(1): 57-80 .

Biggs, D., Courchamp, F., Martin, R. and Possingham, H. (2013). Legal trade of Africa's rhino horns. *Science*, 339:1038-1039.

Brockington, D., Duffy. R. and Igoe, J. (2008). *Nature unbound: Capitalism and the future of protected areas*. Abingdon: Routledge.

Burns, L. Edwards, V. Marsh, J. Soulsby, L. and Winter, M. (2000). *Committee of inquiry into hunting with dogs in England and Wales*. London: HMSO.

Clarke, R.V. and Cornish, D.B. (2001). Rational choice. In Paternoster, R. and Bachman, R. (Eds.), *Explaining crime and criminals: essays in contemporary criminological theory*, Los Angeles: Roxbury.

Conway, E. (1999). *The recording of wildlife crime in Scotland*. Edinburgh: Scottish Office.

Lowther, J., Cook, D. and Roberts, M. (2002). *The international wildlife trade and organised crime: A review of the evidence and the role of the UK*. Wolverhampton: Regional Research Institute, University of Wolverhampton.

Ehrenfeld, D. (2003). Globalisation: Effects on biodiversity, environment and society. *Conservation and Society*, 1(1): 99-111.

Eliason, S.L. (2006). A dangerous job? An examination of violence against conservation officers. *The Police Journal*, 79: 359-370.

Eliason, S. (2003). Illegal hunting and angling: The neutralization of wildlife law violations. *Society and Animals*, 11(3): 225-243.

Elliott, L. (2009). Combating transnational environmental crime: 'Joined up' thinking about transnational networks. In Kangaspunta, K. and Marshal, I.H. (Eds.), *Eco-crime and justice: Essays on environmental crime*, Turin: NICRI.

Fielding, N. and Innes, M. (2006). Reassurance policing, community policing and measuring police performance. *Policing and Society*, 16(2):127-145.

Glenny, M. (2008). *McMafia: Crime without frontiers*. London: Bodley Head.

Hutton, J.S. (1998). Animal abuse as a diagnostic approach in social work: A pilot study. In Lockwood, R. and Ascione, F.R. (Eds.), *Cruelty to animals and interpersonal violence: Readings in research and application*. Indiana: Purdue University Press.

Jasper, J.M. (1997). *The art of moral protest: Culture, biography, and creativity in social movements*. Chicago: The University of Chicago Press.

Joyce, P. (2010). *Policing: Development and contemporary practice*. London: Sage.

Kirkwood, G. (1994). *The enforcement of wildlife protection legislation: A study of the police wildlife liaison officers' network*. Leicester: De Montfort University.

Linzey, A. (Ed.) (2009). *The link between animal abuse and human violence*. Eastbourne: Sussex Academic Press.

Lowe, B.M. and Ginsberg, C.F. (2002). Animal rights as a post-citizenship movement. *Society & Animals*, 10(2): 203-215.

Lowther, J., Cook, D. and Roberts, M. (2002). *Crime and punishment in the wildlife trade: A WWF/TRAFFIC report*. Godalming: WWF-UK.

Marcinkutė, L. (2011). The role of human rights NGO's human rights defenders or state sovereignty destroyers? *Baltic Journal of Law & Politics*, 4(2):52-77.

Martens, K. (2005). Participatory experiments from the bottom up: The role of environmental NGOs and citizen groups. *European Journal of Spatial Development*, 18:1-20.

Marsh, D. and Rhodes, R.A.W. (1992). *Policy networks in British government*. Oxford: Clarenden Press.

Mawby, R. and Yarwood, R. (Eds.) (2010). *Rural policing and policing the rural*. Farnham: Ashgate.

Newburn, T. (2008). *Handbook of policing*. Abingdon: Routledge.

Nurse, A. (2015). *Policing wildlife: Perspectives on the enforcement of wildlife legislation*. London: Palgrave Macmillan.

Nurse, A. (2013a). Privatizing the green police: The role of NGOs in wildlife law enforcement. *Crime, Law and Social Change*, 59(3):305-318.

Nurse, A. (2013b). Species justice: The future protection of wildlife. *The Monthly Journal of the International Green Criminology Working Group*, February 2013.

Nurse, A. (2012). Repainting the thin green line. *Internet Journal of Criminology*, October 2012.

Nurse, A. (2011). Policing wildlife: Perspectives on criminality in wildlife crime. *Papers from the British Criminology Conference*, 11: 38-53.

Nurse, A. (2009). Dealing with animal offenders. In Linzey, A. (Ed.), *The link between animal abuse and human violence*. Eastbourne: Sussex Academic Press.

Nurse, A. (2008). *Policing wildlife: Perspectives on criminality and criminal justice policy in wildlife crime in the UK*. Birmingham: Birmingham City University.

Nurse, A. (2003). *The nature of wildlife and conservation crime in the UK and its public response*. Working Paper No. 9, Birmingham: University of Central England Birmingham, Faculty of Law and Social Sciences.

Parkin, F. (1968). *Middle class radicalism: The social bases of the British campaign for nuclear disarmament*. Manchester: Manchester University Press.

Patten, R., Caudill, J. and Messer, S. (2014). The dirty south: Exploratory research into game warden fatalities in the United States. In Nurse, A. (Ed.), *Critical perspectives on green criminology*. Internet Journal of Criminology, Nottingham: New University Press.

Piquero, A. and Tibbetts, S. (Eds.) (2002). *Rational choice and criminal behavior: Recent research and future challenges*. New York: Routledge.

Roberts, M., Cook, D., Jones, P. and Lowther, D. (2001). *Wildlife crime in the UK: Towards a national crime unit*. Wolverhampton: Department for the Environment, Food & Rural Affairs/Centre for Applied Social Research, University of Wolverhampton.

RSPB (2010). *The RSPB annual review 2009-2010*. Sandy: RSPB.

RSPCA (2007). *Annual review 2006, royal society for the prevention of cruelty of animals*. Horsham: RSPCA.

Schneider, J.L. (2008). Reducing the illicit trade in endangered wildlife: The market reduction approach. *Journal of Contemporary Criminal Justice*, 24(3): 274-295.

Slapper, G. and Kelly, D. (2012). *The English legal system*. Abingdon: Routledge.

Sollund, R. (2013). Animal trafficking and trade: Abuse and species injustice. In Walters, R., Westerhuis, D.S. and Wyatt, T. (Eds.), *Emerging issues in green criminology*. Basingstoke: Palgrave Macmillan.

South, N. and Wyatt, T. (2011). Comparing illicit trades in wildlife and drugs: An exploratory study. *Deviant Behavior*, 32: 538-561.

Stallworthy, M. (2008). *Understanding environmental law*. London: Sweet and Maxwell.

Vold, G. B. and Bernard, T. J. (1986). *Theoretical criminology*: Third Edition. Oxford: Oxford University Press.

Wellsmith, M. (2011), Wildlife crime: The problems of enforcement. *European Journal of Criminal Policy and Research*, 17 (2):125-148.

Wellsmith, M. (2010). The applicability of crime prevention to problems of environmental harm: A consideration of illicit trade in endangered species. In R. White (Ed.), *Global environmental harm, criminological perspectives*. Cullompton: Willan Publishing.

White, R. (2012). NGO engagement in environmental law enforcement: Critical reflections. *Australasian Policing*, 4(2): 7-12.

White, R. (2008a). *A green criminological perspective*. In McLaughlin, E. and Newburn, T. (eds.), *The Sage handbook of criminological theory*. London: Sage.

White, R. (2008b). *Crimes against nature: Environmental criminology and ecological justice*. Devon: Willan.

Wilson, J. Q. (1985). *Thinking about crime*. New York: Vintage Books.

Wyatt, T. (2013). *Wildlife trafficking: A deconstruction of the crime, the victims and the offenders*, Basingstoke: Palgrave Macmillan.

Wyatt, T. (2009). Exploring the organization in Russia far east's illegal wildlife trade: Two case studies of the illegal fur and illegal falcon trades. *Global Crime*, 10(1 & 2):144-154.

Wyler, L. and Sheikh, P. (2013). *International illegal trade in wildlife: Threats and US policy*. Washington: Congressional Research Service.

Zimmerman, M.A. (2003). *The black market for wildlife: Combating transnational organized crime in the illegal wildlife trade*. Vanderbilt Journal of Transnational Law, 36(5):1657-1689.

5

Public Perceptions of Poaching Risks in a Biodiversity Hotspot: Implications for Wildlife Trafficking Interventions

Meredith L. Gore, Michigan State University, USA
Jonah Ratsimbazafy, Groupe d'Etude et de Recherche sur les Primates de Madagascar, Madagascar
Andry Rajaonson, Groupe d'Etude et de Recherche sur les Primates de Madagascar, Madagascar
Amanda Lewis, Utah State University, USA
Jessica S. Kahler, Michigan State University, USA

Introduction

Increased globalization of illicit trade in natural resources can threaten the efficacy of sustainable development, deprive developing economies of billions of dollars in lost revenue opportunities, and fuel socio-political conflict (Brashares et al., 2014). The widespread trafficking of wildlife and forest resources, in particular, can play a central role in financing organized crime and non-state armed groups including terrorist cells, and are increasingly seen as serious international crimes necessitating international policy interventions. Groups engaged in wildlife crime can spread collusive corruption and threaten national security interests, corporate investments, and trade (Nellemann et al., 2014). The United Nations recently identified wildlife and timber trafficking as an international 'environmental crime crisis' due to the pace, sophistication, and scale of the problem (Nellemann et al., 2014). The gravity and high policy prioritization of the issue is evidenced in part by a 2013 United States (US) Presidential Executive Order acknowledging environmental crimes (EC) undermine efforts in development assistance and threaten national security. Also, for example, in January 2015, legislation was introduced in the US to consider wildlife trafficking under federal racketeering and organized crime laws (US Senate, 2015). Finally, defence of natural resources, particularly wildlife, was the first issue whereby CITES, World Customs Organization, Interpol, World Bank, and the United Nations Office on Drugs and Crime worked together on a common goal (e.g. 2010 International Consortium for Combating Wildlife Crime).

These policy initiatives and bilateral agreements make calls for a risk management response to wildlife trafficking, including deterrence, enforcement, compliance, and prevention; activities designed to strengthen and synchronize all levels of the enforcement pyramid (e.g. persuasion, civil penalty, license revocation) (Braithwaite, 1992) but particularly coherent policy and behavior change interventions. The ability of these strategies to reduce wildlife trafficking requires better understanding of the causes and consequences of human behavior that underlie EC activities, particularly related to risk perception.

We know risk perception can influence different group's behavioural decisions about ECs, EC crime control, and EC-related behavior change. In one study, Gore and Kahler (2012) deduced divergent perceptions in how groups (e.g. men, women, decision-makers) characterized risks to wildlife and livelihoods; however, not only were identified risks to wildlife (e.g. poaching) dissimilar in some instances, descriptions of risks varied as well. Gendered differences in risk perceptions signalled different priorities or incentives to participate in efforts to resolve poaching-related risks. Thus, although shared goals and interests may seem to be an obvious reason for cooperative risk management in wildlife management, it is not always obvious that goals are shared. Results revealed opportunity exists to move beyond thinking about gender as an explanatory variable for understanding how different groups think about participating in EC reduction activities. In a complimentary study, Kahler and Gore (2012) explored factors influencing noncompliance with wildlife rules, including those related to poaching; findings illustrated study participants' motivations to comply were not necessarily equivalent to participants' motivations for non-compliance and promote thinking about these two concepts as two sides of the same coin. They found a divergence in opinion when it came to how well decision-makers have taken into account risks to livelihoods and risks to wildlife when creating anti-poaching rules. A majority (68.1%, n = 79) believed poaching risks to wildlife versus human livelihoods (41.4%, n = 48) was weighted more heavily in the decision-making process. In Kahler, Roloff and Gore (2013), participatory field methods were used to garner intelligence from local people involved in community-based natural resource management and policing. Areas with documented poaching events did not spatially correspond to those areas perceived by stakeholders to have high poaching risks. The positive relationship between where stakeholders perceived poaching was occurring and where they believed wildlife was abundant, particularly near national park boundaries, was consistent with local perceptions that poaching activities are motivated by financial gain, meat, and trophies (Kahler & Gore, 2012). These studies indicate the necessity of identifying local prioritization of risks to livelihoods and wildlife before perceptions of risk response can be contextualized.

Although the global community appears to be in general agreement that commercial wildlife trafficking is fuelling an acute need for improved risk-reducing strategies, smart regulation, and more effective enforcement, little to no insight exists about how or what local people think about the topic. Unfortunately, we know little about risk perception associated with risk responses of the phenomenon of EC; a fuller understanding is necessary to design and further strengthen smart regulations and the enforcement pyramid at all levels, as well as general initiatives related to crime prevention and enforcement. If deploying EC-reduction policies and promoting more effective sustainable development are EC regulatory objectives, it is essential to understand local people's perception of environmental risk. Risk perception affects compliance behavior and therefore is essential to regulatory design. Knowledge about EC-related risk perception is crucial for improving risk communication, building capacity, designing effective institutional and regulatory systems, and evaluating interventions. This need is particularly acute in 'biodiversity hotspots' or species-rich areas where rates of wildlife and forest resource exploitation surpass sustainable levels. Biodiversity hotspots are the conservation corollary to crime hotpots, and are used by the conservation community to prioritize research, resources, and policy activities (Brooks et al., 2002).

Wildlife Crime in Biodiversity Hotspots

As one of the world's hottest biodiversity hotspots, with 75% of species being endemic (i.e., found no place else on Earth), Madagascar's flora and fauna face numerous anthropogenic risks such as illegal logging and unsustainable commercial hunting (Goodman & Benstead, 2005; Schwitzer et al., 2013). Three-quarters of Malagasy live in poverty; only 35% have access to an improved water source, and the Gross National Income of $420 USD/year ranks Madagascar 178 of 184 nations. Madagascar has been rated as having extremely high rates of EC and natural resource trafficking, particularly wildlife and timber products (Barrett & Ratsimbazafy, 2009; Schwitzer, Mittermeier, Johnson, Donati, Irwin, et al., 2014). Considering its relatively small land area compared to other countries, it is remarkable that Madagascar is estimated to supply 2.5% of the world's live reptile trade and has one of the highest rated trade volumes in the world (Robinson et al., 2015). EC and wildlife trafficking in Madagascar are at least in part a function of extremely rare species in high demand, corruption, high poverty rates, poor governance, and prolific natural resources (Gore et al., 2011; Nellemann et al., 2014). In particular, especially since experiencing a political crisis in 2009, Madagascar has experienced an upsurge in magnitude and extent of illegal harvesting of endangered hardwoods (e.g. rosewood – Dalbergia spp.) and wildlife trafficking for the global pet trade (e.g. ploughshare tortoise – Astrochelys yniphora) (Duffy, 2010).These foreboding trends paint a bleak picture for Madagascar's degraded environments (Tyson, 2000) and the people whose well-being depend on it (Barrett & Ratsimbazafy, 2009). Because many of the wildlife involved in trafficking originate in biodiversity-rich developing countries such as Madagascar, insights from research conducted there may have practical implications for other biodiversity hotspots around the world. In Madagascar and elsewhere, poaching can be a highly localized activity that directly feeds into the global wildlife trafficking supply chain. Indeed, wildlife poaching is the initial activity upon which trafficking is based. In contrast to other goods and services that are trafficked (e.g. guns, drugs), once wildlife is poached, the effects are permanent and irreversible – the species is either dead or the physical act of trafficking renders the individual animal unfit to return to the wild.

Reducing risks to biodiversity and local livelihoods from wildlife trafficking in Madagascar and elsewhere is a high priority (Schwitzer et al., 2013). Various institutions address wildlife crime and conservation risks in Madagascar, including the fokonolona, or a group of people living within the same village or Malagasy indigenous community (Ratsimbazafy, Gore & Rakotoniaiana, 2013). Fokonolona may, for example, create and enforce rules and sanction offenders independently from but in concert with the federal government. Madagascar also has provincial and federal-level protected areas that may create and enforce wildlife trafficking rules.

In Madagascar, as elsewhere, many conservationists use prioritization schemes based on principles of risk assessment. For example, the International Union for the Conservation of Nature creates 'Red List Categories' formulated according to an objective analysis of extinction risk ranging from 'Extinct' to 'Not Evaluated', as discussed in Schwitzer et al. (2013). Biologists seek to produce more complete datasets on species depending on extinction risk, for example some reptile groups, particularly those associated with fresh water and marine habitats which are facing disproportionately high extinction risks (Böhm et al., 2013); the idea being that more cogent risk assessments will improve conservation actions. These, and most other risk management approaches, are overwhelmingly based on expert analysis of technical intelligence or privileged access to information – not public perception. Understanding public perceptions of risk is of paramount importance to the EC equation because EC is fundamentally about public behavior and behavior is affected by risk perception (Gore et al., 2008). It is well known the potential for experts and publics to perceive risks differently (Lazo, Kinnell & Fisher, 2000). Publics and experts may not consider the same general risks; for example experts may focus on risk of species extinction from wildlife exploitation and publics focus on risk of childhood malnutrition from not exploiting wildlife for protein. Or, laypeople may focus on feeling safe while using public transportation during their daily commute to work while experts focus on emergency preparedness and disaster recovery capacity (Jenkin, 2006). Experts and laypeople may hold alternative views about risks to biodiversity from trafficking, for example experts may consider population-level risks of extinction over the long-term whereas publics focus on short-term localized changes in wildlife abundance. Experts may prioritize management resources based on risk rankings whereas publics base preferences on feeling (Slovic et al., 2004). Groups may not concur about factors influencing the causes of risk exposure nor attitudes about risk management. If not resolved, these differences may pose intractable barriers to resolving negative wildlife trafficking impacts.

In this paper, we posed three research questions based on theories of risk perception(e.g. Slovic, 2000) and designed to provide a coarse baseline about local perceptions of poaching risks vis à vis poaching risks delineated by experts. Our data is not intended to represent a generalized measure of public opinion, nor does it capture local motivations or behavior to exploit natural resources. We do not assume a priori that local publics consider ECs to pose risk to biodiversity, or even that publics consider biodiversity exploitation to be a crime according to the rule of law or rules in use (Robbins et al., 2009). Our research questions are intended to offer preliminary insight about what local publics think about expert approaches to managing risks from wildlife poaching, an EC of highest global concern (Nellemann et al., 2014). This information can inform development and implementation of more smart regulation and different levels of the enforcement pyramid (e.g. enforcement, training and guidance, partnership formation).

Our first research question was: How do local people rank poaching risks relative to risk posed by other environmental hazards? Although experts have diverse and current sources of data upon which to base EC regulations, local people rarely have statistical evidence or police intelligence on hand when they evaluate risks (Slovic, 2000). People respond to risks they perceive, will have strong aversion to certain risks, and be indifferent to others. Rating poaching risks relative to other activities and hazards ensures conservation decisions and actions can be appropriately prioritized. Importantly, the priority given to environmental problems depends on the presence of other existential threats that are not necessarily connected to the environment (Carmi & Bartal, 2014). Conservationists and the enforcement community may rate wildlife trafficking risks as very high policy priorities, but what do local people think? Our second research question was: What factors influence local risk perceptions associated with poaching? Risk perception is a function of many factors, such as knowledge about risk exposure, feelings of dread associated with exposure, voluntariness of exposure, and catastrophic potential of exposure. Factors associated with wildlife-related risk perception are well delineated (e.g. Gore et al., 2007; Muter, Gore & Riley, 2013). Effecting factors influencing poaching-related risk perceptions through a combination of policy, communication, or education, can be a key component of successful wildlife trafficking policy. However, factors influencing expert risk perceptions may not mirror those influencing local risk perceptions.

Our third research question was: What are local perceptions about the types of regulatory responses to poaching risks? Wildlife trafficking may be addressed in myriad ways. Social organizational models of risk, based on cultural theory, provide a typology of regulatory responses to wildlife trafficking risks (e.g. Douglas, 1966,1982). According to cultural theory, four types of people are concerned about different forms of risk and hold specific views of risk responses (Ojasalo, 2009; Thompson, Ellis & Wildavsky, 1990). People from a hierarchical culture are concerned with risks related to law and order and individualists view risks as opportunities unless the risk threatens the free market or their personal freedom. Egalitarians are concerned with technological and environmental risks and risks that will inflict danger on many people or future generations while fatalists do not address risk because they consider it inevitable and outside their control (Ojasalo, 2009; Rippl, 2002). In theory, these distinct approaches to risk influence how these cultural types understand nature

(Thompson et al., 1990; Rippl, 2002). Thus, regulators may craft responses that embrace poaching risks as opportunities for profit or technological innovation, ignore poaching risks because they do not know how to react, reject risks in an effort to actively deter them, or adapt to risks through experimental regulations and control efforts (Douglas, 1978). Characterizing perceptions of regulatory response to poaching risks deepens insight about how local people may respond to proposed EC policies or activities designed by experts using analytical methods and intelligence (Lidskog & Sundqvist, 2013).

Methods and Analysis

Based on five years of collaborative risk perception-based research and teaching experience on poaching in Madagascar as well as social science field experiences in Kenya, Madagascar, Namibia, and the US, we used semi-structured interviews with Malagasy residents, December 2013, to answer research objectives using a five-member research team consisting of three female Americans and two male Malagasy individuals. Our study site was the broader Analamazaotra Special Reserve region of east central Madagascar (Figure 1). We selected Analamazaotra based on our collective

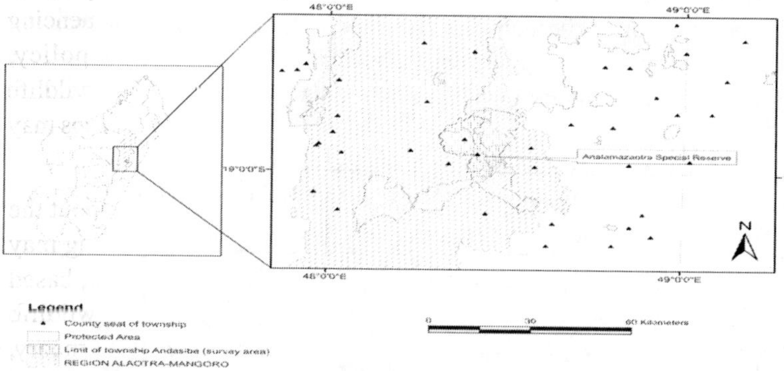

Figure 1: Map of study area within the Analamazaotra Special Reserve, east-central Madagascar

knowledge about EC in Madagascar, permission of relevant traditional authorities, willingness of communities to participate, available research resources, and accessibility. Within Analamazaotra, we used purposeful sampling to intentionally recruit participants at least 18 years of age within eight villages who had experience with the central concepts of our research questions and achieve maximal variation to capture diverse perspectives

(Creswell, 2008). Our approach was intended to capture as much detail as possible about the complex phenomena of EC in Madagascar (Creswell & Plano Clark, 2011). Interviews were conducted primarily in Malagasy with some French and English, to accommodate dialectical variation based on ethnicity, and promote high translator autonomy. Prior to commencing data collection, three Malagasy conservation researchers independently reviewed the interview guide for content validity and salience (Trochim, 2001). In-field instrument translation from English into Malagasy, which occurred during round-table discussions between the research team, resulted in a verbal consensus on translation of the questions. To maximize our capacity to conduct statistical analysis on risk-perception data, we used a visual four-point scale to measure all questions except a risk-ranking question where participants organized individually laminated and labelled photographs of environmental hazards into a meaningful hierarchy. Additional information about methods and measurement are discussed in Gore & Kahler (2015).

After defining study objectives, introducing visual aids to participants (Gore & Kahler, 2015), discussing affiliation, anticipated research outcomes, intended use of data, and definitions of key issues in interviews (e.g. commercial poaching versus legal hunting), informed consent was obtained. Interviews had two parts, a relative risk-ranking activity where participants were asked to hierarchically arrange photographs of eight environmental risks (see Table 1 for eight environmental risks) and semi-structured

Table 1: Malagasy study participants living the Analamazaotra special reserve (n = 28) comparatively ranked eight environmental risks, December 2013.

					95% confidence interval	
Environmental Risk	***Malagasy term***	***Mean ranking***	***t statistic***	***df***	***Lower***	***Upper***
Cyclone	Rivodoza	5.17	10.817*	27	3.96	5.82
Deforestation	Tavy	5.12	9.981*	27	3.72	5.64
Poaching	Fitrandrahanatsyaradalana	5.11	13.427*	27	4.18	5.68
Fire	Dorotanety	4.87	9.43*	27	3.66	5.7
Mosquitos	Moka	4.54	10.824*	27	3.7	5.44
Logging	Kapakapa	4.25	9.836*	27	3.02	4.62
Erosion	Lavaka	4.09	10.785*	27	3.24	4.76
Development	Fandrosoana	4	8.572*	27	3.21	5.22
* p < 0.000						

interview questions. Semi-structured interview questions focused on ranking risk perceptions associated with poaching, factors influencing perceptions of risk, perceptions of responses to poaching risks, effects of poaching risks, and socio-demographics (e.g. age, ethnicity, number of children, profession, sex). Because we were interested in capturing participant opinion about expert approaches to EC management, our questions were more structured than open-ended. Responses were recorded on paper and entered into SPSS version 20 for analysis.

Summated indexes were created for risk perceptions, risk responses, and risk effects with alpha values > 0.65 (Vaske, 2008). We used nonparametric versions of a general linear model (Type III Sum of Squares) to explore variables influencing risk perception. Results cannot be generalized beyond study participants, be used for theory building, or considered a reliable estimate of EC frequency or magnitude; results do provide a novel estimate of how participant perceptions map onto expert-based EC-related risk management approaches (e.g. Nellemann et al., 2014). Michigan State University's Committee on Research Involving Human Subjects (IRB# x10-394) reviewed and approved methods used in this research. Additional information was gathered about cross cultural issues in conservation social science data collection and best practices used to minimize potential sources of bias from Gore and Kahler (2015).

Result

We conducted 49 interviews and encountered two refusals, indicating some participants were willing and able to say no to foreign researchers, a potential source of bias (Trochim, 2001); not all participants answered all questions. One third of respondents were female (n = 16; male n = 33, 66%); average age was 40.9 years (range = 19-77). At least six ethnic groups were denoted in our sample, with Betsimisaraka (n = 28, 56%) and Bezanozano (n = 13, 26%) most commonly represented. Respondents reported an average of 4.5 children and a range of zero to 12. The mean length of time residing in the area was 28.8 years (range = 1 -77 years). Respondents reported 13 different professions, with farmer (n = 27, 54%) and local guide (n = 5, 10%) most frequently noted.

Our first research question focused on how poaching risks rated relative to other environmental hazards of concern to risk managers. Of the eight risks presented, cyclones were rated most and urban development rated least risky; poaching was rated third most risky (Table 1). When asked about the frequency of poaching in their area, respondents (n = 47) reported a wide range of occurrence (no = 15, 30%; low = 14, 28%; middle = 7,

14%; high = 11, 22%). Respondents were not asked about specific species of plants or animals poached in the area although some volunteered examples (e.g. Madagascar boa, which is trafficked for the pet trade).

Our second research question aimed to ascertain attitudinal factors affecting poaching-related risk perception. We explored eleven exogenous factors: familiarity, worry, volition, tampering with nature, novelty, understanding, trust, frequency, management response, cause, and technology were regressed against cognitive risk perception (i.e. perceived probability or likelihood of risk), affective risk perception (i.e. perceived feeling or acceptability of risk), and environmental risk perception (i.e., summation of cognitive and affective risk perception) (Gore et al., 2007; Muter et al., 2013; Sjoberg, 2000 for additional information on variable definition and measurement). General linear model analysis revealed varying influence of these independent variables on environmental risk perception (Sum of Squares=13.52, $df=11$, $R2=.499$, $F=2.718$, $p<.05$), cognitive risk perception, or perception of risk likelihood (Sum of Squares=13.692, $df=11$, $R2=.434$, $F=2.029$, $p<.05$), and affective risk perception, or perception of risk acceptance (Sum of Squares=15.681, $df=11$, $R2=.550$, $F=3.334$, $p<.05$). Tampering with nature was the most influential significant variable in all models tested (respectively, standardized beta coefficients=.381, $p< .05$; .628, $p< .05$; 0.351, $p< .05$).

Our final research question explored the ways in which respondents perceived four different regulatory responses to poaching (i.e. adapt, deter, embrace, ignore). Of the 45 respondents who answered this set of questions, the majority reported deterrence as being the most common regulatory risk response ($n = 27$, 54%) overall. When asked specifically about how different regulatory authorities (i.e., Madagascar National Parks, fokonolona, village, family) respond to poaching risks, deterrence was most commonly reported. The majority of respondents disagreed with the assertion that the fokonolona, village, and family ignored poaching (54% in the case of the fokonolona and 58% in the instances of the village and family). Respondents overwhelmingly disagreed that embracing risk was an appropriate regulatory response for Madagascar National Parks, the fokonolona, their village and their family (Table 2).

Discussion

Natural resource-related crimes, particularly poaching being the root of commercial wildlife trafficking, have settled into the limelight of global policy priorities. Dedicated global consortiums, bilateral and multilateral

Table 2: Malagasy study participants living the Analamazaotra special reserve's December 2013 (n = 42) attitudes about the appropriateness of different institutional responses to local poaching risks

	Institution able to respond to risk							95% confidence interval	
Risk Reponse	Madagascar National Parks	Fokonolona	Village	Family	Overall	t-statistic	df	Lower	Upper
Adapt	16%	12%	6%	8%	5%	9.72*	29	4.4	6.74
Embrace	6%	2%	2%	2%	10%	6.536*	11	3.04	6.13
Ignore	10%	10%	6%	8%	16%	7.419*	24	3.12	5.52
Reject	58%	38%	36%	32%	54%	13.068*	42	6.35	8.67

* $p < 0.000$

agreements, international working groups, grant opportunities, special journal issues, and graduate school-level training on EC barely existed a decade ago. Today, EC is recognized by diverse actors as being a key driver and denouement of social conflict at a global scale (e.g. Brashares et al., 2014). Regulation and enforcement are essential components of wildlife trafficking reduction strategies; the efficacy and efficiency of these strategies is hampered by a lack of understanding about local people's risk perception about the topic. Characterizing public perceptions of risk associated with EC can inform the design, implementation, and evaluation of smart regulation. Further, such insight helps situate poaching within local people's broader threat matrix. In this research, we posed three research questions about public perceptions of poaching risks. Results have implications for local conservation efforts in Madagascar and potentially management of other ECs (Milledge, 2007), particularly wildlife trafficking interventions.

The most noteworthy finding from this study is the characterization of regulatory risk responses from study participants, or the answer to our third research question. Cultural theories of risk propose individuals choose what they fear in relation to their way of life, or, the culture they belong to. Preferences for regulatory responses to risk can be tied to risk perception; four different risk-based prototypical cultures are fatalists, hierarchists, individualists and egalitarians (Rippl, 2002). Sociologists of risk acknowledge public perceptions of acceptable risk and risk regulation are cultural constructs; the selection of dangers is correlated with social organization (Douglas, 1982). Although our data did not measure culture directly, it did capture products of relational processes. Some cultural theorists agree it is possible to learn about social processes from individual-level analysis (e.g. Rippl, 2002).

Our study data are consistent with social groups tending to be egalitarian in nature. Cultural theorists tell us egalitarians have high interest in and are supportive of group efforts, but dislike social relations that are shaped by differences or hierarchic structure. That our results are consistent with this proposition is unsurprising since: (a) the Betsimisaraka, a key ethnic group represented in our sample, are considered to be one of the most decentralized groups within Madagascar (Cole & Middleton, 2001) and (b) the strong role of culture in conservation among Malagasy is well known (e.g. Jones, Andriamarovololona & Hockley, 2008). However, we know that among decentralized groups, social relations are open to negotiation and are assumed to oppose risks that will inflict irreversible dangers on many people or future generations. As a group, egalitarians generally distrust risks that are forced on them by the decisions of a small elite of experts, scientists, or regulatory authorities (Rippl, 2002). If our results about egalitarian views on regulatory responses to risk are confirmed through replication, they suggest an important implication for regulatory approaches aimed at reducing EC such as poaching (Rippl, 2002) for discussion of strengths and weaknesses of different methods for measuring cultural types). Specifically, perceptions about risk regulation among local people may not mirror perceptions of regulators when regulators are educated and socialized to risk-related regulatory strategies in foreign countries. A lack of reflexivity in the perceptions of risk regulation among regulators and local people, just like any expert-layperson divide in perceived risk, is likely to inhibit effective deployment of effective risk-reducing strategies (Gore et al., 2006). For example, lately, the transportation and logistics sector has become involved in strategies to reduce wildlife trafficking; results herein have implications for the feasibility, or lack thereof, of local people responding favourably to increased regulation of the transportation sector (Guest Blogger, 2015).

A second insight from this work stems from knowledge about cultural theory, which suggests shifting regulatory discourse away from the causes and effects of EC to the choice between regulatory authorities to better uncover the components of the EC risk function relevant to local people (Douglas, 1982). Such crystallization is evidently needed, as poaching rates for myriad species continues to increase. In South Africa, for example, home to over 80% of the world's rhinoceroses, poaching increased from less than 1 animal a month in the mid 2000s to an average of 2 animals a day in 2012 and approximately 4 in 2013; 2014 rhino poaching rates surpassed 2013 rates (South African Department of Environmental Affairs, 2014). Reorienting the risk regulation conversation may help engender persuasive effects at the local level; persuasion at this scale is foundational to the enforcement pyramid. For example, the egalitarian Maasai baraza of East Africa, or a meeting of respected male elders and interested members of the community, have determined seasonal grazing patterns for cattle and levied decisions for other localized issues since pre-colonial times. Compared to federal level authorities, the baraza has at times been considered to be a more effective regulatory system than federal regulatory regimes (Western, 1994).

Third, this research builds upon the risk management principle that the first issue in any policy debate about risks and their regulation is to agree on which risks are most worrisome (Douglas, 1982). Clearly, extinction and its deleterious effects on ecosystems and human well-being are paramount risks to conservation scientists and criminal justice officials

(Schwitzer et al., 2014). Risks to society from ineffective wildlife crime control are a central concern of criminologists (Gibbs et al., 2010). Although our study results are not generalizable to the region or country at large, study respondents did not rank poaching as being as risky as natural resource hazards such as cyclones. That 'expert' and 'layperson' perceptions of poaching risks differ in general is not surprising (e.g. Kahler, Roloff & Gore, 2013). What is novel is that data herein offer a first attempt at defining how a key group – local Malagasy people – thinks about this issue, information that with replication can serve as a baseline for bridging the gap via regulatory policy or intervention (Jurin, Rousch & Danter, 2010).

Our study results about risk ranking may be interpreted within the notions of observed memory (e.g. Cole, 2001) and future orientation on risk perception (e.g. Carmi & Bartal, 2014). These phenomena can play an important role in influencing perceptions of poaching-related risks relative to other threats that are more existential, tangible and proximate because risks that are perceived as being temporally closer receive cognitive precedence over others that are perceived as less urgent (Carmi & Bartal, 2014). And, how individuals and groups remember the past can influence their current and future responses to and trust in authorities. Although our study did not explicitly ask questions about Madagascar's 2009-2013 political crisis and transitional government (Ploch & Cook, 2012), the significant changes in food and environmental security, deforestation and degradation, and suspension of donor aid associated with the transitional government undoubtedly influenced participants' perceptions. At a minimum, the effects of the political crisis on participants' perceptions of poaching risks – and how local people may respond to poaching risk regulations – can be interpreted within the context of memory observed (e.g. role of colonial powers and international conservation organizations in conservation) and future orientation (e.g. weighting of poaching risks relative to the existential risks of food and environmental insecurity).

Finally, the notion of tampering with nature is increasingly relevant to understanding environmental risks such as EC; tampering with nature has been found to be a primary driver of individual's risk perception in diverse risk regulation contexts including nuclear power (Sjoberg, 2000). Importantly, the idea may include risks being 'natural' versus 'unnatural', humans and their behavior negatively affecting nature, humans disturbing the order of nature, acting in opposition to nature, or illustrating arrogance toward nature. Beliefs associated with tampering with nature have demonstrated high explanatory power when considered vis à vis issues of technology (e.g. nanotechnology, genetically modified organisms) (Sjoberg,

2000). Again, although our results are not generalizable to a broad population, they suggest tampering with nature can be locally relevant to conservation contexts such as poaching in a biodiversity hotspot. In this regard, the practical implications for managing poaching in biodiversity hotspots may be similar to managing other risks such as climate change: focusing conservation and enforcement policy on individuals' beliefs about technology, health, and environment may be a more effective and efficient strategy for engendering behavior change than attending to other variables such as trust in decision makers tasked with managing poaching risks, controlling poaching risks through enforcement or monitoring, or increasing knowledge about risk through public education initiatives. Among our study participants, local-level institutions such as the fokonolona may be best positioned to manage poaching risks and enforce rules (Ratsimbazafy et al., 2013) because they fit within the egalitarian cultural view of risk response and study participants' opinions about tampering with nature. Ultimately, the relationship between social institution, risk perception, and behavior change is an empirical question that merits additional testing.

Worldwide, wildlife trafficking is the second largest form of black market commerce, behind drug smuggling and before arms (Deeks, 2006). Bleak statistics and trends portend an upward battle for the conservation criminology community in reducing negative effects of poaching and other ECs on biodiversity hotpots and people that depend on them (Golden, 2009; Gutierrez-Velez & MacDicken, 2008). Conservation social science can make a significant contribution to the development, implementation, and evaluation of conservation policy designed to reduce wildlife trafficking in biodiversity hotspots such as Madagascar. Defining and characterizing local people's risk perceptions provides essential baseline data for predicting the acceptability of conservation policies, directing stakeholder engagement initiatives, and targeting resources efficiently. Coupling data about poaching-related risk perceptions with ecological assessments may also enhance outcome assessments and police intelligence by expanding the suite of criteria available for evaluation(Ferraro & Pattanayak, 2006). Risk perception effects conservation behavior and affecting human behavior is essential for reducing wildlife trafficking.

References

Barrett, M.A., & Ratsimbazafy, J. (2009). Luxury bushmeat trade threatens lemur conservation. *Nature*, 461(7263): 470.

Braithwaite, J. (1992). Reducing the crime problem: a not so dismal criminology. *Australian & New Zealand Journal of Criminology*, 25: 1-10.

Brashares, J. S. et al. (2014). Wildlife decline and social conflict. *Science*, 345: 376-378.

Brooks, T. M. et al. (2002). Habitat loss and extinction in the hotspots of biodiversity. *Conservation Biology*, 16: 909-923.

Böhm, M. et al. (2013). The conservation status of the world's reptiles. *Biological Conservation*, 157: 372-385.

Cole, J. (2001). *Forget colonialism? Sacrifice and the art of memory in Madagascar*. Berkeley: University of California Press.

Cole, J. & Middleton, K. (2001). Rethinking ancestors and colonial power in Madagascar. *Africa*, 71: 1-37.

Douglas, M. (1966). *Purity and danger: An analysis of the concepts of pollution and taboo*. London, England: Routledge.

Douglas, M. (1978). *Cultural bias*. Paper no 35, London: Royal Anthropological Institute of Great Britain and Ireland.

Douglas, M. (1982). Introduction to grid/group analysis. In P. Kegan (Ed.), *Essays in the sociology of perception*. London: Routledge.

Duffy, R. (2010). *Nature crime: How we're getting conservation wrong*. New Haven, Connecticut: Yale University Press.

Ferraro, P. & Pattanayak, S. (2006). Money for nothing? A call for empirical evaluation in biodiversity conservation. *PLos Biology*, 4(4): e105.

Gibbs, C. et al. (2010). Introducing Conservation Criminology. *British Journal of Criminology*, 50:124-144.

Golden, C.D. (2009). Bushmeat hunting and use in the Makira forest, north-eastern Madagascar: a conservation and livelihoods issue. *Oryx*, 43: 386-392.

Goodman, S.M. & Benstead, J.P. (2005). Updated estimates of biotic diversity and endemism for Madagascar. *Oryx*, 39: 73-77.

Gore, M.L. (2011). The science of conservation crime. *Conservation Biology*, 25: 659-661.

Gore, M. L. & Kahler, J. S. (2012). Gendered Risk Perceptions Associated with Human-Wildlife Conflict: Implications for Participatory Conservation. PLoS ONE, 7, e32901.

Gore, M. L., & Kahler, J. S. (2015). *Using visual scales in researching global human dimensions of wildlife*. Human Dimensions of Wildlife.

Gore M.L., et al. (2006). Stakeholder perceptions of risk associated with human-black bear conflicts in New York's Adirondack Park campgrounds: Implications for theory and practice. *Wildlife Society Bulletin*, 34.

Gore, M.L. et al. (2007). Factors influencing risk perception associated with human-black bear conflict. *Human Dimensions of Wildlife*, 12: 133-136.

Gore, M.L. et al. (2008). Evaluating a conservation investment designed to reduce human-wildlife conflict. *Conservation Letters*, 1:136-145.

Guest Blogger (2015). *Transportation and logistics sector joins fight against wildlife trafficking*. Retrieved from http://annamiticus.com/2015/01/28/transportation-logistics-sector-joins-fight-wildlife-trafficking/.

Gutierrez-Velez, V.H. & MacDicken, K. (2008). *Quantifying the direct social and governmental costs of illegal logging in the Bolivian, Brazilian, and Peruvian Amazon. Forest Policy and Economics*, 10:248-256.

Jurin, R.R., Roush, D. & Danter, J. (2010). *Environmental communication*. Dordrecht: Springer.

Jones, J. P. G., Andriamarovololona, M. M., & Hockley, N. (2008). The importance of taboos and social norms to conserva-tion in Madagascar. *Conservation Biology*, 22(4): 796-986.

Kahler, J. S. & Gore, M. L. (2012). Beyond the cooking pot and pocket book: factors influencing noncompliance with wildlife poaching rules. *International Journal of Comparative and Applied Criminal Justice*, 35:1-18.

Kahler, J.S., Roloff G. & Gore, M.L. (2013). Poaching risks in a community-based natural resource system. *Conservation Biology*, 27:177-186.

Lazo, J. K., Kinnell, J. C., & Fisher, A. (2000). Expert and layperson perceptions of ecosystem risk. *Risk Analysis*, 20:179-193.

Lidskog, R. & Sundqvist, G. (2013). Sociology of Risk. In S. Roeser et al. (Eds.), *Essentials of Risk Theory*. Springer: Dordrecht.

Milledge, S.A.H. (2007). Illegal killing of African rhinos and horn trade, 2000-2005: The era of resurgent markets and emerging organized crime. *Pachyderm*, 43: 96-107.

Nellemann, C. et al. (2014). *The environmental crisis-threats to sustainable development from illegal exploitation and trade in wildlife and forest resources*. A UNEP Rapid Response Assessment: United Nations Environment Programme and GRID-Arendal.

Ojasalo, J. (2009). Risk, cultural theories, and global management. *The Business Review,* 14: 83-91.

Ratsimbazafy, J. et al. (2013). Community policing in Madagascar. In M. K. Nalla & G. R. Newman (Eds.), *Community policing in indigenous communities*. Florida: CRC Press.

Rippl, S. (2002). Cultural theory and risk perception: a proposal for a better measurement. *Journal of Risk Research*, 5:147-165.

Robbins, P. et al. (2009). Conservation as it is: illicit resource use in a wildlife reserve in India. *Human Ecology*, 37: 559-575.

Robinson, J. E. et al. (2015). Dynamics of the global trade in live reptiles: Shifting trends in production and consequences for sustainability. *Biological Conservation*, 184: 42-50.

Schwitzer, C. et al. (2013). *Lemurs of Madagascar: A strategy for their conservation 2013-2016*. Gland: IUCN Species Survival Commission, Primate Specialist Group.

Schwitzer, C. et al. (2014). Averting Lemur Extinctions amid Madagascar's Political Crisis. *Science*, 343: 842-843.

Sjoberg, L. (2000). Perceived risk and tampering with nature. *Journal of Risk Research*, 3: 353-367.

Slovic, P. (2000). *The perception of risk*. London: Earthscan Publications Ltd.

Slovic, P. et al.(2004). Risk as analysis and risk as feelings: Some thoughts about affect, reason, risk, and rationality. *Risk Analysis*, 24: 311-322.

South African Department of Environmental Affairs (2014). *Update on rhino poaching statistics*. Retrieved from www.environment.gov.za/mediarelease/rhinopoaching_statistics_17jan2014

Thompson, M., Ellis, R. & Wildavsky, A. (1990). *Cultural theory*. Boulder: Westview Press.

Trochim, W.M.K. (2001). *The research methods knowledge base*. Ithaca: Atomic Dog Publishing.

Tyson, P. (2000). *The eighth continent: Life, death, and discovery in the lost world of Madagascar*. New York: Peter Tyson.

Vaske, J.J. (2008). *Survey research and analysis: Applications in parks, recreation and human dimensions*. State College, Pennsylvania: Venture Publishing, Inc.

Western, D. (1994). *Natural connections: Perspectives on community-based conservation*. Washington, DC: Island Press.

6

Monkey Business: The Illicit Trafficking in Barbary Macaques

Daan van Uhm, Willem Pompe Institute for Criminal Law and Criminology, The Netherlands

Introduction

Over the past decades we have become increasingly aware of the growing impact that human activity has on nature. The immense global defaunation[1] has led to the reduction and disappearance of many species (Dirzo et al., 2014). Perhaps one of the most famous examples is the decline of the *Hominoidea* family, i.e. Great Apes, with the exception of Homo sapiens. Currently chimpanzees, orang-utans, gorillas and bonobos are believed to be on the brink of extinction (Stiles et al., 2013). One of the most important dangers to the survival of these species is the illegal trade in wildlife, an illegal business that may be comparable with the drug and weapon trade in profits ranking between $9 and $20 billion annually (Barber-Meyer, 2010; Wilson-Wilde, 2010). These high gains have attracted criminal networks and organized crime in several parts of the world (Zimmerman, 2003; Europol, 2011; Interpol, 2012; van Uhm, 2012a; Sollund & Maher, 2015).

Besides the well-known Great Apes, a lesser-known monkey species, the Barbary macaque (Macaca sylvanus), is at least as threatened with an estimated wild population of around 5,000-6,000 individuals (Majalo et al., 2013). Again, it is the illegal trade that drives these animals to the edge of extinction (van Lavieren, 2008; Waters, 2011; Radhakrishna et al., 2013). Remarkably criminologists neglected to study illegal wildlife markets for a long time (Wyatt, 2009). According to South (2004) the plundering of the earth's natural resources has not been recognized as a crime until recently.

Only from the 2000s onwards, during the emergence of green criminology, a small number of criminologists started to focus on illegal wildlife trade (Zimmerman, 2003; Warchol, 2004; Schneider, 2008; Pires, 2012; Sollund, 2013; Wyatt, 2013). This article aims to contribute to green criminological research on wildlife trafficking by discovering who is involved in the illegal trade in Barbary macaques, how they do it and where this business takes place. First the article will cover the methods used to collect primary data and secondary data. Further the article elaborates on the development of the legislation and the history of the illegal trade. Continuously the structure, organization and modus operandi of the illegal business are discussed followed by a discussion.

Method

The primary research carried out for this article was part of a doctoral research on the illegal trade in wildlife[2]. A multisite research model[3] was used, based on semi-structur0ed interviews, with 24 people directly or indirectly involved in the illegal trade in the main source country Morocco. The method of semi-structured interviews was chosen due to the fact that it accommodates flexibility (Decorte & Zaitch, 2010), which allows specific issues to be addressed in more detail with a clear focus on the organization, trade route and modus operandi of the illegal trade. During my fieldwork, I engaged in participant observations and stayed in areas where wildlife was known to be poached (e.g. Azrou, Ifrane) and in trading markets (e.g. Marrakesh, Tangier) to interview my informants and observe the process. In these areas, I established relationships and met my informants involved in the illegal trade.

Eventually, two hunters in Azrou, nine traders in Marrakesh, Tangier, Oujda, Azrou and Nador, two ex-traders in Azrou, two ex-smugglers in Azrou and Nador, one intermediary in Fez, two guides in Cascades d'Ouzoud and Fez, one primate scientist in Teìtouan and five animal traders were interviewed in different Moroccan cities. These respondents were collected by the method of snowball sampling; the future participants were recruited from among their acquaintances and through the first point of access (Goodman, 1961). The interviews were conducted between March and April 2013 and provided key information about the illegal trade. To maintain anonymity of my informants no names are mentioned in this article.

To strengthen the primary data, secondary data of confiscations in the EU were obtained from the European Union Trade in Wildlife Information eXchange database (EU-TWIX). Each year member states provide their wildlife seizures to be recorded in this database. Subsequently, confiscation data from CITES Belgium, France, Italy, the Netherlands and the Spanish 'Seprona Guardia Civil' have been obtained. This quantified only a part of the illegal trade as a large part of the trade is unreported or undiscovered, the so-called dark number (Coleman and Moynihan, 1996). Law enforcement experts estimate that no more than 10% of all contraband of wildlife is seized (Stiles et al., 2013).

History, Decline and Regulation

Barbary macaques have been associated with humans for thousands of years. They have been found mummified in Egyptian pyramids (Goudsmit & Brandon-Jones, 1999) and petrified in Pompeii (Bailey et al., 1999). Barbary macaques were kept as pets by ancient Romans and Greeks (Hughes, 2003) and were frequently found in early Etruscan art (McDermott, 1936). According to Sax (2001) the word 'monkey' may be first used to refer to Barbary macaques in Europe. In the medieval period, they were desired animals among nobility (Sax, 2001). Illustrations of Barbary macaque at Iron-Age Navan Fort in Northern Ireland (McCormick, 1991) and fossils in Carrickfergus, representing imported domestic pets, have been found (Taub, 1978). Keeping animals as pets was spread from the aristocracy to the middle and lower class citizens during the 16th century (Thomas, 1984). Shakespeare's references to monkeys were probably linked to Barbary apes that were kept as pets by Italian courtesans (Kantha, 2014). The initial introduction of Barbary macaques in Europe (Gibraltar) was probably by the Moors who occupied southern Iberia and kept them as pets (Jackson, 1987). Consequently, the knowledge about apes in European literature during 1700-1900s was mainly based on Barbary macaques (O'Flaherty & Shapiro, 2002). From the 1960s and 1970s on, the popularity of keeping monkeys as pets increased and Barbary macaques were for sale in department stores (e.g. 'Harrods' in London) all over Europe (e.g. Bierman & Smith, 2000; Sanglim, 2014). However, social and moral norms changed and the trade became regulated in an answer to the substantial decline of the species in previous decades.

In historic times, the Barbary macaque was an inhabitant of parts of Europe and virtually all of North Africa (Lindburg, 1980; Camperio Ciani, 1986), but its current distribution is restricted to small relict patches of forest in the rocky and mountainous parts of the Rif and Atlas Mountains (Morocco) and parts of the Tellian Atlas (Algeria) (Camperio Ciani, 1986; Ménard & Vallet, 1993; Scheffrahn et al., 1993)[4]. The total population decreased from an estimated 21,500 individuals in 1974 (Taub, 1977; Taub, 1978) to 15,000 in the 1990s (von Segresser et al., 1999), 10,000 in 2003

(Camperio Ciani, 2003; Modolo et al., 2005), and 5,000-6,000 in 2009 (Majolo et al., 2013). It is estimated that the decline rate has exceeded 50% over the last three generations and this decline is expected to continue in the future (Butynski et al., 2008). While the main threat is habitat loss (Camperio et al., 2005), the illegal trade in Barbary macaques for the pet trade has become one of the greatest threats to the survival of the species (Radhakrishna et al., 2013). Especially from the late 1990s, substantial amounts of Barbary macaques were illegally traded from Morocco to Europe for the pet industry (van Lavieren, 2008)[5].

The Barbary Macaque is classified as 'endangered' on the Red List of Threatened Species and has been listed in Appendix II of CITES[6] and Annex B of the EU Wildlife Trade Regulation (EC 338/97) (Butynski et al., 2008). Consequently, Barbary macaques are prohibited to be imported without proper documents and since 2000 the European Community suspended imports from Morocco and Algeria since trade was deemed to have a harmful effect on the species' status (Article 4.6b of EC Regulation 338/97) (Butynski et al., 2008). In Morocco and Algeria capturing, possession, sale and hunting are prohibited, with an exception for possession of Barbary macaques for cultural purposes at the Djeema el Fna square in Marrakesh through a certificate of ownership (Royaume du Maroc, 2012).

The Beginning of a Lucrative Business

The history of trade in macaques in the late 20th century is mainly related to the demand for laboratory animals. Up to the mid-1970s large numbers of Rhesus macaques (Macaca mulatta) were imported into Europe for the production of the polio vaccine, until a significant decline in the population made a large replacement necessary by crab-eating macaques (Macaca fascicularis) (Mack & Mittermeier, 1984). Still, 80% of the traded CITES mammals consisted of macaques for medicinal purposes during 2001-2010 (CITES trade database, 2013). In the past Barbary macaques were also obtained from the wild for biomedical research. However, hunters misused the obligated certificates to catch additional macaques for the pet trade. According to a former hunter in Azrou 'This was the beginning of the large-scale illegal trade in Barbary macaques. Sometimes ten monkeys were captured, among them only one was needed for biomedical research, and nine was sold in the pet industry' (personal communication, March 15, 2013). The demand for monkeys can be characterized by the affection humans have by 'owning' a monkey. Primates are regularly integrated in human family life and wear clothes, sleep in cribs and eat at the dinner table (Laufer, 2011).

From the late 1990s onwards, sanctuaries and zoological parks in France, Belgium, Spain, Italy and the Netherlands started to notice a substantial increase in the number of Barbary macaques being offered to shelters, after being seized by law enforcement authorities. The majority of these monkeys probably originated from the wild and was destined for the pet industry (van Lavieren, 2008). Based on confiscations in the EU, this trend continued in the 2000s with the Barbary macaque being the most seized CITES mammal in the EU, accounting for almost 25% of live mammal-related seizures during 2001-2010. Within this ten-year period, 86% of 49 EU seizures of 55 Barbary macaques occurred in Spain with 90% originating from Morocco and 8% from Algeria. The average number of smuggled Barbary macaques is one monkey per confiscation (N=49; M=1.1; SD=0.3) and most were confiscated in Spain due to a lack of CITES documents (van Uhm, 2016a; van Uhm, 2016b).

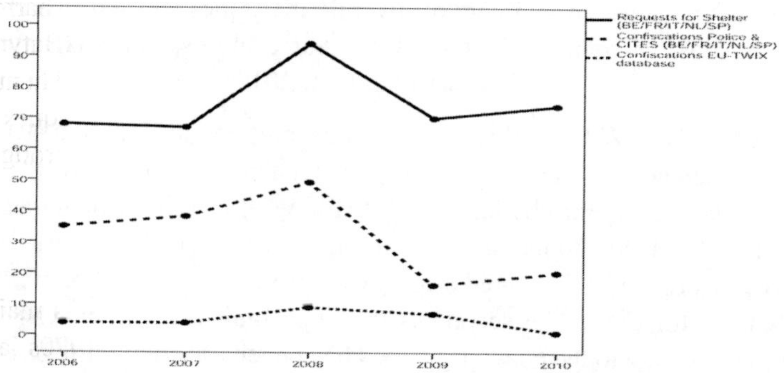

Figure 1: Confiscations and shelter requests

However, the actual numbers of seizures are much higher based on data from CITES Belgium, France, Italy, the Netherlands and the Spanish 'Seprona Guardia Civil' – only between 2006-2010, 159 Barbary macaques were confiscated. Simultaneously, 219 requests to shelter Barbary macaques occurred[7]. Figure 1 presents similar trends of seizures and requests for shelter with a peak in 2008.Several (former) hunters and illegal traders in Azrou and Oujda recognized this trend with numbers as high as 500 to 600 Barbary macaques traded illegally from the Azrou area in the late 2000s (personal communication, March 15, 2013; personal communication April 27-29, 2013). If we assume that 10% of the illegal monkeys are seized (Stiles et al., 2013), indeed around 500 Barbary macaques (±50 confiscated animals) were illegally traded in 2008 and then around 200 Barbary macaques may be traded nowadays. The decline from 2008 onwards is possibly caused by the economic crisis in Europe (traders, personal communication, March 15 and April 27-29, 2013).

Poaching and trafficking macaques

The first step in the operation is poaching of the Barbary macaques. According to multiple respondents, Azrou and its surroundings (Middle Atlas in Morocco) is the center of the illegal trade in Barbary macaques (trader, personal communication, March 13, 2013; trader, personal communication, April 24, 2013; BMC, personal communication, April 25, 2013)[8]. The season for poaching starts in spring (April) because there are many infant monkeys. A poacher in Azrou explains: 'There is a demand for young monkeys for two reasons. First, young monkeys get used to people better than older ones and, secondly, they are easier to smuggle in suitcases or bags' (personal communication, April 29, 2013). This may explain the significant decrease in numbers of juvenile macaques and females in the Middle Atlas between 2007 and 2009 (Haut Commissariat aux Eaux et Forêts et à la Lutte Contre la Désertification, 2012).

According to Wyatt (2013) there may be three generic kinds of poachers. The first category is the subsistence poacher who lives in or nearby the poaching area. They poach illegal wildlife for personal use (without trading) or money involved. Bongerian criminologists would label it as 'crimes to survive'. Bonger (1932) linked crimes with poverty based on bread prices and arrests for theft. The second is the opportunistic poacher who also lives in proximity to the poaching area. They poach illegal wildlife because the opportunity is available, not necessarily due to economic profits (Wyatt, 2013). Pires (2012) found that situational incentives in the context of environmental factors play an important role in illegal wildlife trade, such as parrot poaching and illegal fishing. In contrast to the subsistence and opportunistic poacher, the specialist poacher is calculated in their capture. They sell it to middlemen or at the market to gain economic profits (Wyatt, 2013). The illegal poaching is often a well-considered choice driven by high profits, low risks and minimal sentences (Schneider, 2008).

The poachers are usually relatively poor local specialists from Berber villages in the Azrou area in Morocco. This region is home to Morocco's earliest inhabitants, the Berber tribes, who have been living on herding for centuries (Wagner, 1993). They live in small villages in the middle or around the cedar forests (personal observation, March 15 & April 28-29, 2013). While situational incentives may play an important role (e.g. they live near the poaching area), they catch monkeys in particular on demand by middlemen or tourists driven by economic gains. The poachers anticipate quickly on the orders and can even deliver more than 10 monkeys a week on short notice. They usually work in groups of four to eight people. Three poaching methods to capture the monkeys have been described by (former) poachers (personal communication, March 15, 2014; personal communication April 29, 2013):

- Hunters (6-7 people) isolate female macaques with infants from the group with trained dogs. They goad them from the dense forest into a solitary tree, then saw the branches and harass the mother with sticks and stones, until the babies are dropped.
- Hunters place grids on the ground and wait until macaques walk over them. They then pull on a rope that is connected to a net that hangs from trees and it falls to the ground so that the monkey is caught in the net.
- Hunters entice Barbary macaques with fruit or coconuts until they are close enough to catch them.

Regularly, guides, lumberjacks and forest rangers are involved and receive a 100 Dirham (±€10) commission if they refer potential buyers. Moreover, agreements are made with other local people to poach outside the tourist spots in the Cedar Forest so as not to disturb the financial benefits from tourism (poacher, personal communication, April 29, 2013; middleman, personal communication, March 14, 2013).

Based on my observation, monkeys are sold directly along the side of the road, but usually middlemen *semsar* organize the business. According to Wyatt (2013) middlemen are key individuals in smuggling operations moving wildlife along a network. They buy wildlife from the poacher and transfer them to wildlife markets (Warchol, 2004). Middlemen arrange a smuggler to stay at a hotel in Azrou meanwhile poachers do their job for anywhere between €50-100 per monkey: 'within two days we can arrange their order and then they go back to resell the monkeys in Tangier, Oujda or Marrakesh' (personal communication, April 29, 2013). The transport of the monkeys from the forests to the trade hubs in Morocco (e.g. Tangier, Marrakesh) requires a certain degree of sophistication. The monkeys may be hidden in the trunk of the car or additional actors like bus drivers or police officers are involved. For instance, one modus operandi between Azrou and Oujda is as follows: one person gets on the bus in Azrou and registers suitcases or bags, with monkeys hidden inside, as checked-in baggage and then gets off the bus at the second or third stop, while leaving the luggage on the bus. If the bus is held for a police check and they find the macaques, the bus driver has an alibi, because he has a receipt for the suitcases or bags that have been 'forgotten' by the traveller in question. Without a police check, the bus arrives in Oujda where someone else will pick up the suitcases or bags with the monkeys and the bus driver is then paid (former smuggler, personal communication, April 28, 2013; bus driver, personal communication, April 29, 2013). According to the people in the trade, communication between hunters, middlemen and traders generally proceeds by mobile phone. One seller at the famous Djeema el Fna Square in Marrakesh underlined that the use of mobile phones is relatively safe as prepaid cards can be easily bought and changed without registration (personal communication, March 13, 2013).

Relatively large numbers of Barbary macaques are offered for sale (€200-250) by traders in several large Moroccan cities. For instance, a trader in Tangier explained during our meeting: 'I just sold one monkey yesterday, but there are two more for sale (...) Different people work for me to catch the monkeys in Azrou and then I keep the monkeys in my house in Tangier city. On Monday a European guy with a lorry will pick up three ordered monkeys' (personal communication, April 25, 2013). Simultaneously another trader in Tangier sold a macaque to a European lady and showed later that day pictures of a larger macaque for sale (personal observation, April 25, 2013). These domestic traders are often animal traders involved in legal and illegal animal trade. Symbiotic interrelation between the under- and upper world are not uncommon. This collaboration between animal traders and middlemen or poachers is effective due to mutual benefits (Passas, 2002). The interdependence is characteristic in the illegal trade in wildlife (e.g. Cook et al., 2002; Naylor, 2004; Lyons & Natusch, 2011). The informal market is much more integrated in Morocco than in the West (Ilahiane and Sherry, 2008). The *souks* stand in sharp contrast to the Western industrial model of doing business whereby different types of trading intertwine. Though, legal animal traders use opportunities to trade in Barbary macaques illegally to earn additional profits. While in Morocco the price for a monkey increases during the process from the poacher (€50-100), intermediaries (€120-150) to the trader (€200-250), the discrepancy between prices in Morocco and the EU is considerably higher with a tenfold increase from € 200-250 to € 2000.

Crossing the Ocean

The Strait of Gibraltar seems to be the natural border between Morocco and Spain. However, the presence of Spanish territory (Melilla & Ceuta) on the north Moroccan coast represents an important factor in its status as a 'smuggler's paradise'. For long time smuggling has been a part of life in the northern Rif of Morocco. Especially since the human population almost doubled during 1960-1970, smuggling, of every item imaginable, was booming (McMurray, 2001; Parnell & Kane, 2003). For example, people have become specialized in smuggling goods from Nador to Melilla (McMurray, 2001).

However, smuggling live animals differs substantially from smuggling wildlife products such as ivory or rhino horn. To hide live monkeys and to keep them alive during the smuggling process requires systematic planning and logistics (Stiles et al., 2013). Because the smugglers aim to limit the period of time in transit to ensure the survival of the monkey, the route is mostly scheduled and appointments have been made between actors in the smuggling process. For this reason, the smugglers prefer to transport the monkeys directly to the trader or buyer, without secondary activities (personal communication, April 27, 2013; personal communication, April 28, 2013).

Young Barbary macaques are usually hidden in suitcases or bags under a car seat and incidentally on the body[9]. Several dealers confirmed that to keep the macaque quiet and to decrease the macaque's stress levels, the monkeys are anesthetized with a sleep aid for children, *n3as*, which can be bought from a regular pharmacy (personal communication, March 17, 2013; personal communication, April 26, 2013; personal communication, April 27, 2013; personal communication, April 29, 2013). 'The syrup makes them sleep. Then you put the small monkey in a suitcase under the seat of your car and cross the border to enter Spain' (personal communication, April 27, 2013). This syrup can anesthetize the monkey for up to 16 hours during the border crossing. This is more than enough since the boat ride lasts a mere 45 minutes. According to a trader in Tangier: 'If police stops you, you just say it is a present for a friend to show that it is not a structural business (…) of course you should hide the monkey, but if they catch you and they see it is not organized business they let you go' (personal communication, April 24, 2013).

Although most seizures (> 85%) include one Barbary macaque (van Uhm, 2016b), certain cases contain large quantities. In 2012, six Barbary macaques were confiscated at the border between Hungary and Serbia (MPC, 2012). Opportunistic small-scale traffickers or tourists smuggle usually one Barbary macaque hidden in suitcases or bags in their car and cross the border by ferry to the EU. Incidentally, tourists smuggle the monkeys by aircraft where they are hidden in checked-in baggage (EU-TWIX database, 2013)[10]. More organized forms of smuggling could include more anesthetized monkeys hidden in cars or trucks. Additionally, there may be collaboration with legal actors such as lorry drivers and custom officers. A trader in Marrakesh explains his symbiotic relationship with a lorry driver who uses his legitimate trade to hide monkeys and, secondly, with custom officers that can be bribed around 200 to 500 Dirham (€20-50) (personal communication, March 17, 2013). If custom officers cannot be bribed, there is always a chance that they do not want to confiscate monkeys, out of a lack of priority or no shelter being available (BCM, personal communication, April 25, 2013).

The Monkey Route

Due to its strategic location and relatively close intercontinental border crossing, Morocco is well known as the main port between Africa and the EU for the illegal drugs trade (cocaine, heroin, cannabis and synthetic drug precursors) and migration (UNODC, 2006; Europol, 2011; Carpenter, 2012), as well as the illegal wildlife trade (Highfield & Bayley, 1996; Cowdrey, 2002). Out of 22,205 seized wildlife shipments in the EU between 2001-2010, the majority originates from Africa with Morocco on the top of the African list (612 illegal shipments), in which the Strait of Gibraltar operates as a gateway for illegal wildlife from Africa to the EU. Regularly spur-thighed tortoises (Shipp, 2002; Znari et al., 2005), Mediterranean chameleons (Bergin & Nijman, 2014), African grey parrots and Barbary macaques (van Lavieren, 2008; Waters, 2011) are traded from Morocco, confirmed by seizures (van Uhm, 2016a). Already in the mid-1990s, Interpol (1996) noticed that Morocco is an important origin and transit country for illegal wildlife.

The illegal trade in Barbary macaques starts usually from the Azrou area in Morocco with structured orders (4-10 monkeys every two months) from Tangier, Marrakesh, Oujda, Casablanca and Fez for the retail trade (Figure 2). A (former) trader estimates that around 200 macaques are captured in the Azrou area for primary trade to the EU each year (personal communication, April 29, 2013). The major portion of the monkeys is transferred to Tangier where ferries depart every 45 minutes to Algeciras and Tarifa in Spain. Several traders arrange for macaques on demand, even more than 50 annually (personal communication, April 24, 2013). At Djeema el Fna square in the heart of Marrakesh approximately 10 Barbary macaques are present daily for entertainment and sale. Sellers at the square suggested that more than 30 macaques are sold each year at this square alone (personal communication, March 13; 16-18, 2013). Oujda, near the Algerian border is another trade hub from where 50-80 monkeys are sold each year and then are smuggled via Melilla to Spain, France and probably Italy (trader, personal communication, April 27, 2013; convicted drug smuggler, personal communication, April 28, 2013). Casablanca and Fez do have relatively small markets; however, there are still possibilities to arrange macaques by intermediaries (middleman, personal communication, March 14, 2013). From these trade hubs European traders or tourists smuggle the monkeys by road and ferry through the ports of Tangier, Ceuta and Melilla to Tarifa, Cadiz, Algeciras, Almeria and Alicante in Spain[11]. The Schengen treaty provides unhindered trade to European destination countries (Cowdrey, 2002); especially France, Italy and Spain are major outlets (trader, personal communication, March 15, 2013; trader, personal communication, March 17, 2013; trader, personal communication, April 24, 2013)[12].

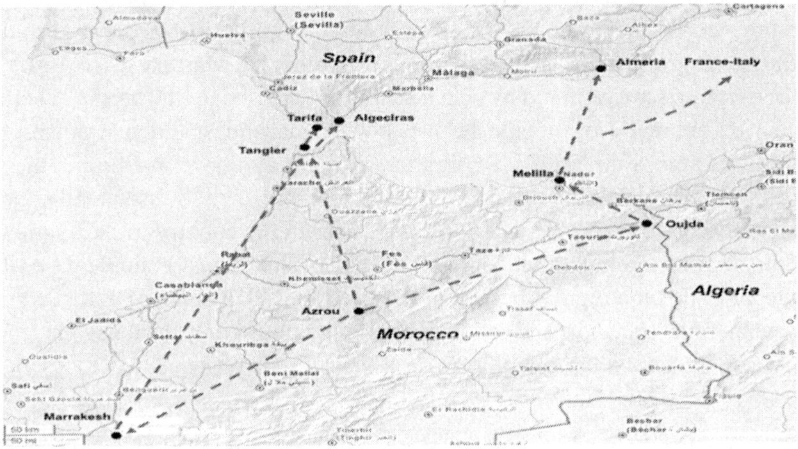

Figure 2. Smuggling routes

Colliding Criminal Networks in Morocco

Previous research (e.g. van Lavieren, 2008) indicated that the trade in Barbary macaques was loosely based on the tourist industry. Indeed, many respondents in this research referred to opportunists, usually European tourists who buy and smuggle one monkey to keep as a pet back home or small-scale traders who reduce the costs of their holiday by reselling the monkey. According to a trader at Djeema el Fna square in Marrakesh: 'Regularly I sell them to European tourists who fell in love with an infant monkey (...) They would like to keep them as pets or want to rescue them from the use in entertainment' (personal communication, March 17, 2013). This makes sense in the context of the increasing numbers of foreign visitors in Morocco, around 10 million each year, mostly from Western Europe.

According to Esmond & Chryssee (2012) tourists in Morocco are responsible for a substantial illegal trade in live animals and their products.

Nevertheless, criminal networks with a high degree of organization have also been found in the illegal trade in Barbary macaques. Well-organized, semi-loose networks use sophisticated methods to trade large orders of monkeys and earn relatively high profits. The animals are moved along a line of contacts (a chain), where key aspects of the movement may be overseen by one or two central players (Morselli, 2009; Elliott, 2009). The organized traders have a network with several legal and illegal actors to transfer the Barbary macaques various times a year as a financial business. For instance, according to traders in Marrakesh a (criminal) network has recently been established between Moroccan and European traders. Their operations are based on a regular basis with the involvement of three or more people in the chain. Once every two months the entrepreneurial European group gives an order by phone to traders in Marrakesh. In Azrou, the macaques are captured by poachers and transported to Marrakesh, where couriers are ready to smuggle the anesthetized macaques hidden in suitcases in a van across the Strait of Gibraltar. When they arrive in Europe, they call to indicate that the mission has been accomplished. Subsequently, the monkeys are transported to a domestic trader in the country of destination (personal communication, March 17, 2013). This is just a single case of illegal trade on a regular basis that is carried out by a chain of actors who poach, trade, transport and sell animals under control of central key players (see figure 3 for alternative flows).

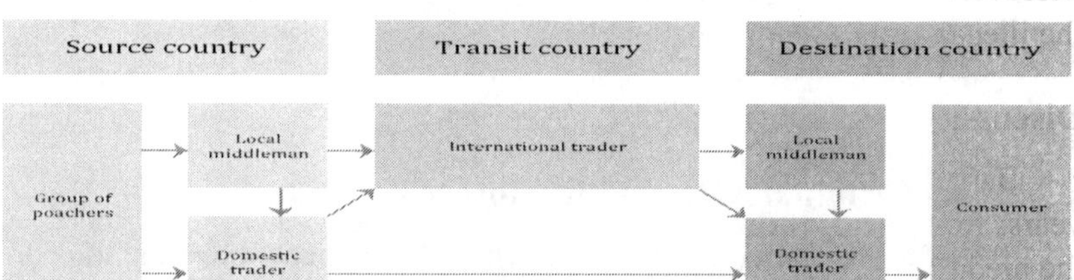

Figure 3. The generic illegal trade

Apparently, there is a regular movement of captured macaques smuggled by road from the rural area of Azrou to urban areas, such as Tangier, Oujda and Marrakesh. From there, direct lines to Europe are organized by different groups of entrepreneurs. The role of a courier between countries in a semi-loose network is demonstrated by a former Spanish smuggler, who was deployed to transfer monkeys multiple times a month from a trader in Tangier (Morocco) to a trader in Algeciras (Spain). Subsequently the animals were transferred to Northern Spain for sale. 'For a period of eight years my friend smuggled monkeys bought in Tangier to a trader in Algeciras (...) At the end he bought a house in Spain with the profits of € 1000 per monkey' (personal communication, April 25, 2013). Each actor has his own task, specialty and profit within this network. A Spanish trader near Barcelona had several monkeys under his supervision in 2008. In these flourishing business times, a consumer could choose between six young macaques (MBC, personal communication, April 25, 2013). While in the trading areas of Tangier and Melilla organized crime related to drug trafficking (e.g. the Tangiers Cartel) has been identified (e.g. UNODC, 2003), the informants did not recognize the involvement of classical Moroccan crime syndicates, *Moroccan Res Kbir*, in the illegal trade in Barbary macaques. However, the degree of organization is visible by the fact that it is even possible for the organizations to enter into a trade agreement to deliver more than 50 monkeys to Europe each year (trader, personal communication, April 24, 2013).

Especially, the high profits and low risks and minimal sentences in the illegal wildlife trade are attractive to criminal networks (Zimmerman, 2003; Schneider, 2008). As mentioned, a Barbary macaque can be purchased for around 2000 Dirham (€ 200) in Morocco and sold in the EU for € 2000 (10 times its original price). Assuming that the profit for the illegal trade in 50 monkeys per year would amount to around € 100,000, the potential profit to be made would be around 42 times the minimum yearly wage by Moroccan standards (US Department of State, 2012). The incentives for the illegal trade are thus obvious.

Discussion

Barbary macaques have been traded and kept as pets for thousands of years; from the ancient Egyptians, Romans and Greeks to the nobility in the medieval period and a more recent fashion explosion in the 1960s and 1970s. Although in the past Barbary macaques were traded legally, in the late 20th century the trade slowly became criminalized. Social and moral norms were subject to change as species became threatened with extinction. Under pressure of several moral entrepreneurs and non-governmental organizations, the trade in endangered exotic animals, such as Barbary macaques, became restricted by regulation (CITES)[13]. Currently, trade in wild Barbary macaques is forbidden without proper documents. The criminalization process proceeded with the prohibition of keeping monkeys as pets in several European countries during the 1990s and 2000s. Belgium,

Bulgaria, Estonia, Hungary, Italy, Latvia, Lithuania, the Netherlands, Portugal, Sweden and Andalucía, an autonomous community in Spain, have implemented bans on the keeping of primates as pets, while Denmark prohibits the import and private keeping of all primates, except marmosets and tamarins. It is likely that other European countries will follow (RSPCA, 2012).

The poachers and traders in Azrou are also more aware of being caught than before. While for a long time the sale of monkeys took place in plain view in Morocco, currently the big deals are made in the late evening to avoid the attention of the police (personal communication, March 15, 2013; personal communication, April 29, 2013). Some of my informants were shocked about the fact that a friend was caught with three monkeys at the bus station in Azrou (personal communication, April 29, 2013). People involved in the trade explained that currently improved and sophisticated methods are required to dodge law enforcement[14]. Nevertheless, the criminalization of the illegal trade is not comparable with other forms of crime, such as drugs or weapons. The plundering of the earth's natural resources is still a widely tolerated process (Stretesky and Lynch, 2014). Regarding the Barbary macaque trade, regularly law enforcers do not confiscate monkeys due to a lack of priority or no shelter being available and serious, large-scale criminal investigations are uncommon, if not completely lacking. According to various illegal entrepreneurs, the border between Morocco and Spain is still quite poorly controlled when it comes to the smuggling of wildlife (personal communication, March 15, 2013; personal communication, March 18, 2013). This is strengthened by a strong belief that the trade is loosely based on the tourist industry.

However, as demonstrated in this study the degree of organization should not be underestimated. The illegal trade in Barbary macaques is carried out by a chain of actors, collectors, traders, middlemen, smugglers, and overseen by one or two central players. These involved networks are driven by situational, rational and cultural incentives. Morocco seems to function as an important source country and transit hub of the illegal wildlife trade from Africa to the EU. The geographic location between two continents with the Strait of Gibraltar as close border crossing underlines the opportunities provided by the infrastructure. Several traders highlighted this geographic advantage for other illegal wildlife trades in Morocco too. Leopard skins are bought in wildlife markets in Mali, rolled in carpets and smuggled through Morocco into the European Union (personal communication, March 13, 2013) and spur-thighed tortoises are collected from the Middle Atlas and smuggled in boxes of 150-200 animals across the border (personal communication, March 17, 2013). Additionally, the relatively low priority by law enforcement, opportunities for corruption[15] and rising prices on the black market are attractive to criminal networks. Since the population of Barbary macaques is as few as 5,000-6,000 individuals left, the price may quickly increase in the near future. Currently prices of other monkeys, such as gorillas, already reached as high as $40,000 (van Uhm, 2012b). However, certain western countries point their finger at 'those' corrupt source countries in Africa (Boekhout van Solinge, 2010). Yet, blaming only the source countries ignores the other side of the market. The trade is dependent on the cultural demand in Europe for extraordinary exotic animals. In Europe, the rarity of a species determines its value on the black market and subsequently the demand (van Uhm, 2014; 2016b). This progressive rarity and the parallel rising value on the black market may be an important driver of overexploitation by illegal entrepreneurs (Courchamp et al., 2006; van Uhm & Siegel, 2016).

Finally, in comparison to other forms of crime, the harms of the trade are significant. As green criminologists do not limit their study of crimes defined by law, harms are included in their research. Moreover, they reject the orthodox anthropocentric perspective of transgressions or harms against humans and include the environment with its biodiversity and non-human species (Beirne and South, 2007; White, 2008; 2011). From this eco-centric perspective the impact of the trade in Barbary macaques is not only reflected from anthropocentric harms, such as potential threat for health in the context of distribution of zoonotic diseases (e.g. Ebola), but also environmental harms may be of relevance (van Uhm, 2015). The estimated illegally traded 200 monkeys each year may have a serious harmful effect on the remaining population, especially due to the focus on youngsters. By poaching infant macaques, the adult population is not adequately replaced (Camperio Ciani & Mouna, 2006). If this trend continues, the population has little opportunity to recover. In addition, in many small populations of endangered species the reproduction and survival is limited by mate shortage or limited genetic variety. This ensures that a small population can extirpate at a higher rate than expected, the so-called Allee effect (Courchamp et al., 2006). In addition, the harms to individual animals are substantial during poaching, trade and at the final destination (Sollund, 2011; Nurse, 2013; Wyatt, 2013). A high stress level is caused during the hunt where dogs are used to attack the monkeys with youngsters, the monkeys are drugged with syrup to smuggle them across the border and to live, if they survive transport, in a human urban environment. Furthermore, the largest population (around 70%) of Barbary macaques lives in the cedar forests in Middle Atlas of Morocco (Camperio Ciani et al., 2005; Mouna et al., 1999). These forests are endangered ecosystems with several endemic and rare plant and animal species[16]. Generally, monkeys play an important role in ecosystems as disseminators of seeds (Wilson, 1993). The Barbary macaque disperse the seeds of many plants (Herrera, 1995; Ménard & Vallet 1996), is prey for golden jackals, red foxes and eagles and host a number of ecto- and endoparasites (Jinn, 2011). From this ecocentric perspective the effect of the disappearance of the Barbary macaque for the cedar forest ecosystem is incalculable.

Conclusion

This article has demonstrated that besides opportunistic tourists and small-scale traffickers, sophisticated semi-structured networks are active in the harmful illegal trade in Barbary macaques from Morocco to the European Union. Yet, in the context of multiple incentives and low priority by law enforcement illegal trade will remain and the future of the small wild population of Barbary macaques is highly debatable. Would in the succession of the Barbary lion and leopard the Barbary macaque, which we have shared a large history; disappear in the cedar forests in the Middle Atlas? Or will effective interventions save the small population from its demise? In any case, it is a race against time to save this ancient species from the edge of extinction.

Notes

1. Defaunation is an equivalent of deforestation and is used to refer to the loss of species, populations and local declines in abundance of individuals of wildlife.
2. The research results are part of the doctoral research 'Uncovering the illegal wildlife trade: inside the world of poachers, smugglers and traders' by Daan van Uhm at Utrecht University.
3. Multi-site research is a qualitative research approach to get in-depth knowledge of a phenomenon that has been barely explored. The researcher uses the same research plan at various local, regional, national or international sites to get an overview of the phenomenon (Siegel, 2009).
4. A semi-wild population of around 200 macaques lives in the Upper Rock Nature Reserve of Gibraltar in Europe.
5. Occasionally the Barbary macaques were used for monkey-fights and as guards.
6. CITES is the Convention on International Trade in Endangered Species of Wild Fauna and Flora, an international agreement between governments that came into force in 1975 to ensure that no species of wild fauna or flora becomes or remains subject to unsustainable exploitation because of international trade.
7. Because rescued macaques are occasionally moved to another shelter in the EU, double counting may explain the higher number of rescued animals compared to seizures.

8. There are indications that the trade is shifting to other parts in the Middle Atlas (e.g. Be└ ni-Mellal).
9. Women may smuggle macaques on the body because they are not searched according to a former smuggler (personal communication, April, 27, 2013).
10. For instance, on a routine check on freight at Zaventem Airport (Belgium) one Barbary macaque from Morocco has been found on 08-10-2010.
11. Based on confiscations in Spain during 2006-2012 the majority of the macaques were captured in the ports of Algeciras (27), Cadiz (14), Alicante (13) and Melilla (10). An alternative former trade line is from Oujda through Oran (Algeria) to Alicante (Spain) and Marseille (France).
12. Barbary macaques were seized in Spain (102), France (28), Belgium (21), Italy (5) and the Netherlands (3) during 2006-2010.
13. While the populations of great apes on the CITES I list, such as chimpanzees (population: 299,700 - 431,100), orangutans (population: 54,000 and 6,600) and bonobos (population: 15,000-20,000) (Stiles et al., 2013), are estimated to have a larger population, the Barbary macaques still remain on the CITES list II. While it is the question if the existing regulatory framework of CITES is the right instrument to prevent species for extinction (Sollund & Maher, 2015), with a very small wild population the Barbary macaque should at least be included in CITES I to save the species from extinction.
14. Note that hunting has been criminalized within people's lifetime.
15. Corruption is a major issue in Morocco (Transparency International, 2009).
16. The last populations of Barbary lion and leopard were seen in the cedar forest ecosystem in the Middle Atlas and there would be still small populations of lynx, hyena and Berber deer. Other mixed cedar forests can only be found in small parts of Lebanon, Cyprus and in Anatolia in Turkey.

References

Barber-Meyer, S. M. (2010). Dealing with the clandestine nature of wildlife: Trade market surveys. *Conservation Biology*, 24(4):918-923.

Bailey, J. F. et al. (1999). Monkey business in Pompeii-unique find of a juvenile Barbary macaque skeleton in Pompeii identified using osteology and ancient DNA techniques. *Molecular Biology and Evolution*, 16: 1410-1414.

Beirne, P. & South, N. (Eds.) (2007). *Issues in green criminology: Confronting harms against environments, humanity and other animals*. Cullompton: Willan publishers.

Bergin, D., & Nijman, V. (2014). Open, unregulated trade in wildlife in Morocco's markets. *Traffic Bulletin*, 26(2): 65.

Bierman, J. & Smith, C. (2000). *Fire in the night: Wingate of Burma, Ethiopia and Zion*. Random House Inc.

Camperio Ciani, A. (1986). La Macaca sylvanus in Marocco: soprav- vivenza o estinzione. Osservazioni personali e dati storico-demog- rafici. *Antropologia contemporanea*, 9 (2): 117-132.

Camperio Ciani, A. (2003). Antropol. *Mediterran*, 1:57-68.

Camperio Ciani, A., Palentini, L., Arahou, M., Martinoli, L., Capiluppi, C. & Mouna, M. (2005). Population decline of Macaca sylvanus in the middle atlas of Morocco. *Biological Conservation*, 121: 635-641.

Camperio Ciani, A. & Mouna, M. (2006). Human and environmental causes of the rapid decline of the Barbary macaque in the Middle Atlas of Morocco. In J.K. Hodges & J. Cortes (Eds.), *The Barbary macaque: Biology, management & conservation*. Nottingham: University Press.

Carpenter, A. (2012, March). *Security and Europe's Sea Ports: Threats and issues facing maritime gateways to Europe*. Paper Presented at the Policing and European Studies Research Conference, Dundee.

Convention on International Trade in Endangered Species of Wild Fauna and Flora (CITES) *trade database,* 2013.

Coleman, C. & Moynihan, J. (1996). *Understanding crime data: Haunted by the dark figure*. Buckingham: Open University Press.

Cook, D. et al. (2002). *The international wildlife trade and organised crime: A review of the evidence and the role of the UK*. Regional Research Institute, Wolverhampton: University of Wolverhampton.

Courchamp, F., et al. (2006). Rarity value and species extinction: the anthropogenic Allee effect. *PLoS biology*, 4(12): e415.

Cowdrey, D. (2002). *Switching channels: Wildlife trade routes into Europe and the UK*. Wolverhampton: University of Wolverhampton.

Decorte, T. & Zaitch, D. (2010). *Kwalitatieve methoden en technieken in de criminologie*. Leuven: Acco.

Dirzo, R. et al. (2014). Defaunation in the Anthropocene. *Science*, 345(6195): 401-406.

Domalain, J. Y. (1977). *Animal connection. Confessions of an animal trafficker*. London: Heinemann.

Drucker, G. R. (1984). *The feeding ecology of the Barbary macaque and cedar forest conservation in the Moroccan Moyen Atlas*. The Barbary Macaque.

Elliot, L. (2009). Combating transnational environmental crime: Joined up thinking about transnational networks. In Kangaspunta, K. & Marshall, I. (Eds.), *Eco-crime and justice: Essays on environmental crime*. Turin: UNICRI.

Endcap (2012). *Wild pets in the European union*. Endcap.

Esmond, M. & Chryssee, P.M. (2012). *Tourists underwrite Morocco's illegal trade in wildlife artefacts*. SWARA.

Europol (2011). *Organised crime threat assessment* (OCTA). The Hague: Europol.

Europol (2013). *Serious and organised crime threat assessment (SOCTA)*. The Hague: Europol.

Fa, J. E. (1983). The Barbary macaque - the future. *Oryx*, 17(02): 62-67.

Fa, J.E. (1984). Habitat distribution and habitat preference in Barbary Macaques (Macaca sylvanus). *International Journal of Primatology*, 5: 273-286.

Fa, J. E., Taub, D. M., Menard, N., & Stewart, P. J. (1984). *The distribution and current status of the Barbary macaque in North Africa*. In The Barbary Macaque. Springer.

Goodall, J. (2014). *Want to raise a chimp? Think again*. Retrieved from website.

Goodman, L. A. (1961). Snowball sampling. *The Annals of Mathematical Statistics*, 32(1):148-170.

Goudsmit, J. & Brandon-Jones, D. (1999). Mummies of olive baboons and Barbary macaques in the Baboon Catacomb of the Sacred Animal Necropolis at North Saqqara. *The Journal of Egyptian Archaeology*, 85: 45-53.

Haut Commissariat aux Eaux et Forêts et a la Lutte Contre la Deìsertification (2012). *Conservation action plan for the Barbary macaque (Macaca sylvanus) in Morocco*. Rabat: Eaux et Forêts.

Herrera, C. M. (1995). Plant-vertebrate seed dispersal systems in the Mediterranean: ecological, evolutionary, and historical determinants. *Annual Review of Ecology and Systematics*, 26:705-727.

Highfield, A.C., & Bayley, J. R. (1996). The trade in tortoise-derived souvenir products in Morocco. *Traffic Bulletin*, 16(1):33-35.

Hughes, J. D. (2003). Europe as consumer of exotic biodiversity: Greek and Roman times. *Landscape Research*, 28(1): 21-31.

Interpol (1996). *Internal report: Noah*. Lyon: Interpol.

Jackson, W. G. F. (1987). *The rock of the Gibraltarians: a history of Gibraltar*. New Jersey: Fairleigh Dickinson University Press.

Jinn, J. (2011). *Ecosystem roles of the Barbary macaque*. University of Michigan.

Kantha, S. S. (2014). *Subhuman primates in Shakespeare's oeuvre*. Current Science, 106(7):1021.

Laufer, P. (2011). *Forbidden creatures: Inside the world of animal smuggling and exotic pets*. Maryland: Rowman & Littlefield.

Lindburg, D. G. (Ed.) (1980). *The macaques: Studies in ecology, behavior, and evolution*. New York: Van Nostrand Reinhold Company.

Lyons, J. A., & Natusch, D. J. (2011). Wildlife laundering through breeding farms: illegal harvest, population declines and a means of regulating the trade of green pythons (Morelia viridis) from Indonesia. *Biological Conservation*, 144(12): 3073-3081.

Mack, D. & Mittermeier, R.A. (1984). *The international primate trade*. Washington, DC: TRAFFIC.

Majolo, B. et al. (2013). Out of Asia: the singular case of the Barbary macaque. In Radhakrishna, S. et al. (Eds.), *The macaque connection: Cooperation and conflict between humans and macaques*. New York: Springer.

McCormick, F. (1991). The dog in prehistoric and Early Christian Ireland. *Archaeology Ireland*, 5(4): 7-9.

McDermott, W. C. (1936). The ape in Roman literature. *Transactions and Proceedings of the American Philological Association*, 67: 148-167.

McMurray, D. (2001). *In & out of Morocco: Smuggling and migration in a frontier boomtown*. London: Minneapolis.

Ménard, N. & Vallet, D. (1993). Population dynamics of Macaca sylvanus in Algeria: an 8-year study. *American Journal of Primatology*, 30: 101-118.

Ménard, N., & Vallet, D. (1996). Demography and ecology of Barbary macaques (Macaca sylvanus) in two different habitats. In Fa, J. E., & Lindburg, D. G. (Eds.), *Evolution and ecology of macaque societies*. Cambridge: Cambridge University Press.

Modolo, L. et al. (2005). Phylogeography of Barbary macaques (Macaca sylvanus) and the origin of the Gibraltar colony. *Proceedings of the National Academy of Sciences*, 102: 7392-7397.

Mouna, M. et al. (1999). *A propos des populations du singt-magot (Macaca sylvan us L) dans le Moyen Atlas.* Proceedings of the First International Conference on Biodiversity and Natural Resources Preservation.

Morselli, C. (2009). *Inside criminal networks*. New York: Springer.

MPC (2012). *6 Barbary macaques confiscated in Serbia*. MPC.

Naylor, R. T. (2004). The underworld of ivory. *Crime, Law & Social Change* 42: 261-295.

Nurse, A. (2013). *Animal harm: Perspectives on why people harm and kill animals*. Farnham : Ashgate Publishing.

Parnell, P.C., & Kane, S.C. (Eds.) (2003). *Crime's power: Anthropologists and the ethnography of crime*. New York: Palgrave Macmillan.

Passas, N. (2002). Cross-border crime and the interface between legal and illegal actors. In van Duyne, P. et al. (Eds.), *Upper world and underworld in cross-border crime*, Nijmegen: Wolf Legal Publishers.

Pires, S. F. (2012). The illegal parrot trade: a literature review. *Global Crime*, 13(3): 176-190.

Radhakrishna, S., et al. (Eds.) (2013). *The macaque connection: Cooperation and conflict between humans and macaques*. New York: Springer.

Royaume du Maroc (2012). *Conservation action plan for the Barbary macaque (Macaca sylvanus) in Morocco*. MPC.

RSPCA (2012). *Primates as pets: Is there a case for regulation*? RSPCA.

Sanglim, S. (2014). *Orde Wingate: A man of genius 1903-1944*. Yorkshire: Pen and Sword Books.

Sax, B. (2001). *The mythical zoo: An encyclopaedia of animals in world myth, legend and folklore*. Santa Barbara, CA: ABC Clio.

Scheffrahn, W. et al. (1993). Ecology, demography, and population genetics of Barbary macaques in Algeria. *Primates*, 34(3): 381-394.

Schneider, J. L. (2008). Reducing the illicit trade in endangered wildlife the market reduction approach. *Journal of Contemporary Criminal Justice*, 24(3): 274-295.

Shipp, A. (2002). Wildlife for sale in Marrakech, Morocco. *Traffic Bulletin*, 19 (2): 65.

Siegel, D. (2009). *The Mazzel ritual: culture, customs and crime in the diamond trade*. New York: Springer.

Sollund, R. (2011). Expressions of speciesism: The effects of keeping companion animals on animal abuse, animal trafficking and species decline. *Crime, Law and Social Change*. 55(5):437-451.

Sollund, R.A. (2013). Animal trafficking and trade: Abuse and species injustice. In Walters, R. et al. (Eds.), *Emerging issues in green criminology: Exploring power, justice and harm*. New York: Palgrave Macmillan.

Sollund, R. & Maher, J. (2015). *The Illegal wildlife trade: A case study report on the illegal wildlife trade in the United Kingdom, Norway, Colombia and Brazil*. A study compiled as part of the EFFACE project. Oslo & Wales: University of Oslo and University of South Wales.

South, N. (2004). The greening of criminology. In Carrabine et al. (Eds.), *Criminology: A sociological introduction*. Abingdon: Routledge.

Stiles, D. et al. (Eds.) (2013). *Stolen apes – the illicit trade in chimpanzees, gorillas, bonobos, and orangutans: A rapid response assessment*. Arendal: UNEP.

Stretesky, P. B. & Lynch, M. J. (2014). *Exploring green criminology: Toward a green criminological revolution*. Farnham: Ashgate Publishing.

Taub, D.M. (1977). Geographic distribution and habitat diversity of the Barbary Macaque (Macaca sylvanus L.). *Folia Primatologica*, 27:108-133.

Taub, D. M. (1978). The Barbary macaque in North Africa. *Oryx*, 14(3): 245-253.

Thomas, K. (1984). *Man and the natural world: Changing attitudes in England 1500-1800*. London: Penguin Books.

US Department of State (2012). *Country reports on human rights practices*. Washington, DC.

UNODC (2003). *Country profile drugs and crime: Morocco*. Vienna: UNODC.

UNODC (2006). *Organized crime and irregular migration from Africa to Europe*. Vienna: UNODC.

van Lavieren, E. (2008). The illegal trade in Barbary macaques from Morocco. *Traffic Bulletin*, 21(3):81-88.

van Uhm, D.P. (2012a). Organised crime in the wildlife trade. *Centre for Information and Research on Organised Crime Newsletter*, 10 (2): 2-4.

van Uhm, D. P. (2012b). De illegale handel in beschermde diersoorten. *Justitiële verkenningen*, 28 (2): 91-100.

van Uhm, D. P. (2014). Criminaliteit en traditionele Chinese medicijnen. *Proces*, 93 (2): 130-143.

van Uhm, D.P. (2015). Towards moral principles regarding non-human animals: a green criminological perspective. In F. De Jong (Ed.), *Overarching views of crime and deviancy. Rethinking the legacy of the Utrecht school*. The Hague: Eleven International Publishing.

van Uhm, D.P. (2016a). Illegal trade in wildlife and harms to the world. In: Spapens, A.C.M. et al. (Eds.), *Environmental crime in transnational context*. Farnham: Ashgate Publishing.

van Uhm, D.P. (2016b). *Uncovering the illegal wildlife trade: inside the world of poachers, smugglers and traders*. Unpublished Doctoral Thesis, Utrecht: Utrecht University.

van Uhm, D.P. & Siegel, D. (2016). The illegal trade in black caviar. *Trends in Organized Crime*, 19 (1): 67-87.

von Segresser, F. et al. (1999). Genetic differentiation within and between isolated Algerian subpopulations of Barbary macaques (Macaca sylvanus): evidence from microsatellites. *Molecular Ecology*, 8: 433-442.

Wagner, D.A. (1993). *Literacy, culture and development: Becoming literate in Morocco*. Cambridge: Cambridge University Press.

Warchol, G. L. (2004). The transnational illegal wildlife trade. *Criminal Justice Studies*, 17(1): 57-73.

Waters, S. (2011). Europe's other primate. *ZooQuaria*, 75: 22-23.

White, R. (2008). *Crimes against nature: Environmental criminology and ecological justice*. Cullompton: Willan Publishers.

White, R. (2011). *Transnational environmental crime: Toward an eco-global criminology*. London: Routledge.

Wilson, E. O. (2002). *The future of life*. New York: Alfred A. Knopf.

Wilson-Wilde, L. (2010). Wildlife crime: A global problem. *Forensic Science, Medicine, and Pathology*, 6(3): 221-222.

Wyatt, T. (2009). Exploring the organization of Russia Far East's illegal wildlife trade: Two case studies of the illegal fur and illegal falcon trades. *Global Crime*, 10(1-2): 144-154.

Wyatt, T. (2013). *Wildlife trafficking: A deconstruction of the crime, the victims, and the offenders*. Hampshire: Palgrave Macmillan.

Zimmerman, M. E. (2003). Black market for wildlife: combating transnational organized crime in the illegal wildlife trade. *The Vanderbilt Journal of Transnational Law*, 36:1657-1689.

Znari, M. et al. (2005). Growth and population structure of the Moorish Tortoise (Testudo graeca graeca) in West Central Morocco: possible effects of over-collecting for the tourist trade. *Journal of Arid Environments*, 62(1): 55-74.

7

Law Enforcement of the Wildlife Trafficking in UK and Norway

Jennifer Maher, University of South Wales, UK
Ragnhild Sollund, University of Oslo, Norway

Introduction

The trafficking of wildlife is increasingly recognized as a serious and organized crime which impacts significantly on the environment, society, economy and security, nationally and internationally (Schneider, 2012; Wyatt, 2013). Increasing international concern is evidenced by the role global (e.g. United Nations, Interpol), and international (e.g. European Commission, International Consortium on Combating Wildlife Crime – ICCWC) entities and consortiums, national governments (e.g. UK) and civil society (e.g. TRAFFIC[1]) have played in bringing together global leaders and stakeholders who have pledged to eradicate IWT. In the past three years alone, high profile events have produced international declarations, resolutions and operations aimed at enhancing political momentum and policy responses (herein referred to as responses) to IWT (e.g. the 2013 Bangkok 16th Conference to the Convention on International Trade in Endangered Species of Wild Flora and Fauna – CITES[2]); the 2014 European Commission (EC) IWT Conference and Workshops; the 2014 European Parliament Resolution on Wildlife Crime; and the 2014 London IWT Conference and Declaration).

Despite this growing concern and apparent demonstration of international political will, IWT is growing fast, suggesting that current responses are inadequate, perhaps lacking understanding of offenders' (including consumers') motivations and how to dissuade and deter. AsYuryFedotov, Executive Director of the United Nations Office on Drugs and Crime (UNODC, (2013:np), suggests: '...in many cases, inadequate laws and sanctions, under-resourced and weak capacities in law enforcement and lack of coordination between competent authorities are being exploited by criminal networks'. Through a SWOT analysis – a framework for analyzing strengths, weaknesses, opportunities and threats - this article aims to advance understanding of current policy responses, identify their limitations, and offer suggestions for improvements. The SWOT analysis is based on a comparative case study on the IWT in the UK and Norway, part of the EFFACE project (Sollund and Maher, 2015). This multi-method qualitative study focused on the IWT (predominantly on terrestrial fauna) in the UK, Norway, Colombia and Brazil[3], and aimed to identify common and unique features of the responses in these four locations, whilst also exploring the various motivations for why people engage in the trade, the nature of the trade, and types of victimization. A key objective of the EFFACE project was to make policy recommendations that built on good practice and addressed shortcomings.

The development of policy recommendations is strongly linked to SWOT analysis[4]. Identified as an effective and objective way to determine how capable a response is when it comes to surviving threats and capitalizing on opportunities, SWOT considers the impact of many different internal and external factors (Dealtry, 1992). SWOT analysis is neither the first nor the last step in the process and must be based on sound knowledge about the present environment and trends. The key literature, against which the strengths and weaknesses are judged, is therefore evaluated first. A brief account of the methodology is presented next, followed by an overview of responses in the case study locations which are discussed and evaluated through SWOT analysis. Conclusions from this analysis are examined in the recommendations section, where a forward analysis of policy opportunities, in line with the green criminology harm perspective, is presented. The focus of the article is thus empirical rather than theory development.

Background

The IWT involves the 'illegal trade, smuggling, poaching, capture or collection of endangered species, protected wildlife...derivatives or products thereof' (Wyatt, 2009: 145). It is currently identified as one of the largest illegal trades worldwide, positioned among the illegal drugs, arms and human trafficking trades in regards to economic value (UNODC, 2012;

Wyatt, 2013). Due to the clandestine character of this trade, weak controls and enforcement, and inconsistencies in recording offences, the scale of IWT is difficult to measure. What is agreed is that IWT is increasing both in quantity and in value (TRAFFIC, 2008). In particular, practices which involve the use of animals in food (e.g. expensive delicacies like pangolin) and medicine (e.g. rhino horn and tiger bone powder) are widespread. This growth is believed to be facilitated by globalization (open borders and an expanded marketplace), the internet, which is said to play a significant role as an intermediary between supply and demand (IFAW, 2008; Interpol/IFAW, 2013; Lavorgna, 2014), and the migration of cultural practices; as witnessed in the EU (van Uhm, 2014).

To place the IWT in an economic context, the legal trade in wildlife has been estimated to be worth from 159-160 billion USD (Duffy, 2010) to over 300 billion USD annually (Lawson and Vines, 2014). The illegal trade has been valued at 20 billion USD (Galster cited in South and Wyatt, 2011). From a harms perspective, each year the IWT results in millions of lost lives, a substantial number of which are killed for their parts or die during capture or in captivity (RSPCA, n.d). The crude and harsh methods by which live animals are trafficked reportedly cause up to 90% loss of life for reptiles and rare birds (Warchol et al., 2003; Sollund and Maher, 2015). Already depleted populations of iconic species (e.g. elephants) are currently being killed at an unprecedented rate. According to Baille et al. (2004), the IWT threatens a third of the world's species. Consequently, and almost impossibly, CITES (2014) currently monitors 35,000 wild species, of which roughly 5,600 animal species are listed as threatened. Growing concern over the loss of biodiversity and the widespread consequences of the trade has generated international political interest and policy responses aimed at eradicating the IWT. However, as long as IWT generates high profits (rhino horn, for example, is worth more than gold) and remains low risk (Europol, 2013; EC, 2014) would-be traders are unlikely to be deterred by current responses.

Beyond the ineffectiveness of deterring human involvement in IWT, policy responses also seem to be failing in considering animal welfare, possibly even offering possibilities for further harm (e.g. euthanasia). Harm (to animals and humans) is a central concept in this case study. The values underlying this analysis are thus consistent with those prevalent in green criminology, such as ecological justice, species justice and environmental justice (Beirne and South, 2007; White, 2013). Green criminologists (Fitzgerald, 2010) acknowledge that animals are victims, not least those traded (e.g. Cao and Wyatt, 2013). This perspective recognizes these victims as individuals with intrinsic value and interests in living unharmed (Regan, 1983). Yet, 'speciesism', a human prejudice and ideology that counteracts the interests of non-human species, facilitates the exploitation and harm of wildlife in many ways – often not in breach of the law. Speciesism is sustained by capitalist and consumerist practices (Stretesky et al., 2013; White, 2013) and is compared to racism and sexism (e.g. Nibert, 2002). However, while speciesism is likely to be a driving force for the IWT and the responses to it, due to the empirical, policy approach of this article, it is emphasized here only in brief and with reference to recommendations.

The foremost support for responses is the CITES convention. It requires Member State parties (there are 181 parties, including the UK and Norway since 1976) to monitor and regulate the wildlife trade through dedicated domestic legislation based on three lists – Appendix I, II and III – which respectively ban, regulate and monitor trade. It is important to clarify that under CITES trade is only banned for critically endangered species; with many species neither listed nor protected by the convention, it has been subject to heavy criticism (Sollund, 2011). And while there is no empirical assessment of CITES, Reeve (2002) argues that although CITES is a flagship wildlife agreement, it is compromised by being a self-policed system with no global enforcement agency to oversee compliance. She suggests the key risks to CITES are the dissolution of borders (making the permit system irrelevant) and chronic underfunding. Furthermore, the study Warchol et al. (2003), among others (Wyatt, 2009; UNODC, 2012; van Uhm, 2014), argues that forgery, fraud and corruption further compromise CITES. For example, trafficking in birds involves various forms of fraud, including forging CITES certificates/permits, 'laundering' illegal with legal birds and under-reporting numbers, selling wild caught birds as locally bred and smuggling birds in air freight. Both the aforementioned Director of the UNODC and John E. Scanlon, Secretary General of CITES, have argued for harsher prosecution and punishment of CITES offences, especially when organized criminal networks are involved. They have highlighted deficiencies in responses to international criminal activity, particularly with regard to legislation, law enforcement, criminal analysis and international cooperation (CITES, 2013). Organized crime within the IWT is a concern also raised by Interpol, Europol, the UN and the EU. According to Europol (2011), the European IWT is, in part, organized by crime groups within the EU. Consequently, there have been moves to categorize the IWT as a serious and organized crime, to encourage a more robust enforcement approach and to punish offenders more severely in 2013 both CITES (at the 16th meeting of the Conference of Parties) and the UN Commission identified the IWT as a serious crime and encouraged Member States to adopt strategies used successfully to tackle other serious crimes (CITES, 2013). Key NGOs and stakeholders also contribute to the enforcement response. In addition to providing data, advice and funding for enforcement agencies (see TRAFFIC, World Wildlife Fund for Nature – WWF, World Animal Protection – WAP); they provide non-enforcement prevention and intervention strategies aimed at helping both human and non-human victims.

IWT in Case Study Locations

UK

The UK comprises four countries: England, Northern Ireland, Scotland and Wales. Although law enforcement has devolved in Northern Ireland and Scotland, many of the agencies responsible for responding to IWT operate across the UK, thus the focus of this article is UK-wide. The annual UK legal wildlife trade has been valued at up to 50 million pounds (Department of Environment, Food and Rural Affairs – DEFRA, 2015) and it is recognized as a major consumer and transit point for the IWT (and to a lesser degree, a source for raptors). Between 2001 and 2010 the EU-TWIX database recorded more than 50,000 confiscations in the EU, many of which were products destined for the Traditional Chinese Medicine – TCM market (van Uhm, 2014). Border Forces (UK customs agency, henceforth called customs) made 509 CITES seizures in 2014, including 23 live animals, 139 animal products, 22 caviar, 14 coral, 39 ivory and 208 TCM preparations (containing animals and/or plants) (Data.gov.uk, 2014). Each seizure represents one incident rather than the actual quantity seized. For example, the 23 live animal seizures totalled 1,289 individual animals. It is seldom easy and sometimes impossible to accurately and precisely quantify the IWT due to the challenges of identifying animals/products. Much IWT stems from demand for luxury products. Products typically reach the UK via sea and air ports through a variety of methods (e.g. holiday souvenirs placed in luggage, items concealed on persons, online purchases via postal packages and items concealed in large freight). Importantly, the EU single market plays a role in the IWT: once wildlife is smuggled into the EU it can move here unchallenged; effectively, the success (or failure) of border responses in other EU countries have serious consequences for UK enforcement.

In response, CITES is implemented at an international level through the EU Council Regulations (338/9745) and nationally through the Control of Trade in Endangered Species [COTES46] (1997 – this legislation is currently under review). The three CITES appendices are divided among four Annexes in the EU regulations and COTES. Annexes A, B and C largely correspond to CITES Appendix I, II and III, but also contain some non-CITES-listed protected species. Annex D includes additional monitored species (EC, 2010). The Customs and Excise Management Act [CEMA47] 1979, the Animal Welfare Act [AWA48] 2006 and the Wildlife and Countryside Act 198149 (and additional wildlife legislation) may also be used in response to IWT offences. EU regulations require the UK to designate one management authority [MA] and at least one scientific authority [SA] to oversee the enforcement of CITES. DEFRA (Wildlife Division), the UKs management authority, is supported by ministerial (Home Office) and non-ministerial departments, government (including the JNCC - scientific authority for animals) and non-government advisors agencies (who coordinate partnership work between statutory agencies and NGOs) and criminal justice agencies (see Figure 1). As many agencies share

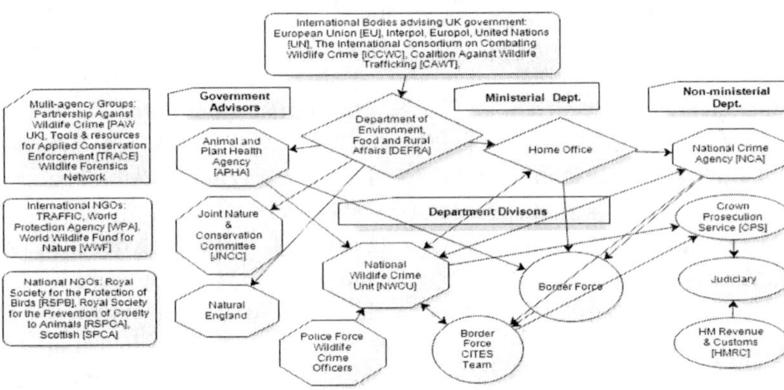

Figure 1

complementary responsibilities in CITES, close cooperation is necessary for efficient and effective regulation and enforcement. The agency responsible for confiscating IWT animals is responsible for their welfare, this may include the disposal (usually rehoming) or non-disposal (return to owner – possible under the Police and Criminal Evidence Act 198450) of these animals. The purpose-built Heathrow Animal Reception Centre [ARC] provides short-term accommodation for all confiscated/seized wildlife. National and international NGOs are also central to the UK response, providing financial support, scientific and welfare evidence and advice, and facilitating public and political education and awareness. There are also many specialist interest groups with a stake (e.g., Taxidermy Law). Despite differences in roles, responsibilities, powers, focus and objectives, all those involved in interrupting, exposing and obstructing IWT work closely together.

Norway

Norway, on the edge of northern Europe, has a long coastline and borders with Sweden, Finland and Russia, and roughly five million inhabitants, of which approximately 750,000 are immigrants or of immigrant descent (Statistics Norway, 2015). A very affluent country due to a large oil industry, Norwegians travel extensively and many have the means to purchase material goods, including wildlife products. It is predominantly a consumer country for IWT (with the exception of raptors, mainly). Consumer practices include those of ethnic minority populations whose cultural practices in wildlife consumption diverge from ethnic Norwegians'. Animals are trafficked to Norway by plane, ferry, car, in luggage, as well as through freight companies. Offenders take advantage of porous borders and try to traffic wildlife (e.g. parrots) with other contraband (alcohol and tobacco) through customs (border-crossing points) with fewer, less regular controls, than at the Svinesund border (a main crossing point between Norway and Sweden).

The Norwegian CITES regulation November 2002 nr. 1976[12] (revised in 2013) is based on the Law of biodiversity[13], The Wildlife Law[14], the Law on Regulation of Importation and Exportation from 6 June 1997[15], Law about Svalbard[16], and the Law about Jan Mayen[17]. Often the Animal Welfare Act[18], with related regulation against the importation, trade and keeping of 'exotic species'[19], is applied in IWT cases. Police and customs variously apply these different laws and regulations (even in their statistics), and whether or not an animal in question is CITES listed is often unclear. This makes it impossible to establish an accurate overview of CITES cases, determine in a given period how many cases involve trafficking of CITES-listed animals, or confirm how such crimes are solved.

Between 2008 and 2014, 1839 animals and animal products were seized, including various parrot and reptile species, Siberian tiger, leopard, brown bear, lion, crocodile and alligator, sea horse, hippo, corals and elephant ivory, according to The Customs Directorate[20]. As in the UK, the quantity of animals seized by far exceeds the number of seizures. Sadly, few CITES cases have been brought to trial in Norway. Most are regarded as misdemeanours rather than crimes, which is one reason why they are not prioritized by police and prosecutors (Svae-Grotli, 2014). Most trafficking cases result in fines spanning from 2000-15000 NOK, though typically less than 5000 NOK (635 USD) (Sollund, 2013a). The police impose fines and if fines are accepted the case will not go to trial.

In Norway, the Norwegian Environment Agency is responsible for CITES and is the formal owner of all wildlife. It is also the agency which is consulted by customs and the police when animals are seized, to establish whether CITES species are involved, to regulate the required permits and to decide the destiny of seized animals. The Food Safety Authority is responsible for animal welfare and care for seized animals, though there are no specific rescue facilities for receiving confiscated CITES animals. If Kristiansand Zoo and the Oslo Reptile Park decline seizures, the animals are commonly euthanized. Økokrim, The Norwegian National Authority for Investigation and Prosecution of Economic and Environmental Crime, is the central unit for investigation and prosecution of such crimes – it responds to 'serious' crimes only – and is the main source of specialist skills for the police and the prosecuting authorities, although there are officers with a specific responsibility for environmental crime in each police district. In practice, most cases are concluded at police district level, through fines.

Method

Case study data were collected by means of semi-structured interviews and observations with experts including NGOs, environmental authorities, law enforcement agents and, in Norway only, offenders. Analysis of penal cases, verdicts and confiscation reports further supplemented these data. Interviews lasting between 1-3 hours were recorded, transcribed and then analyzed using QSR NVIVO software and a grounded theory approach (Glaser and Strauss, 1967). Direct observations in the UK and Norway focused on key agencies responsible for responding to the IWT (e.g. air and port customs and police headquarters). In the UK, unstructured overt observations, with access to restricted areas, were undertaken at four sites over a period of 1-2 days (per site); work processes were observed and discussed with key agents. Both purposive and snowballing sampling techniques were used to identify participants who possessed both first-hand experience with and knowledge of the IWT. A sample of 28 expert interviews (UK: 11, Norway: 12 and 5 offenders) and five observations (UK: 4, Norway 1) was achieved. In Norway, documentary analysis was conducted on 46 customs confiscation reports (for confirmed CITES cases) – in addition to seven CITES verdicts[21] (i.e. CITES was used as an argument and relevant legislation applied).Where possible, these cases were traced through the judicial system to identify how they were prioritized, processed and punished. Although this study cannot identify the prevalence of IWT, nor evaluate the responses from all key stakeholders (every methodology has limitations), the adoption of multi-method, multi-site data collection and multi-agency participation, in addition to the in-depth systematic literature review, delivers robust findings[22].

SWOT analysis was conducted by evaluating the interview and observation data, through which participants were asked questions about their response: what works well (strengths); what causes concern and needs improvement (weaknesses); what else could be done (opportunities); and what are the key challenges (threats). By analyzing participants' answers, SWOT analysis identified how to build on strengths, eliminate weaknesses, exploit opportunities and mitigate the effects of threats (Dealtry, 1992).

Discussion

The SWOT analysis gave rise to a host of issues too numerous to discuss here. This perhaps reflects the complexity of responding to the IWT. The strengths, weaknesses, opportunities and threats that are addressed are summarized in Table 1. It is important to note that strengths and weaknesses are frequently alternative conclusions for the same issues and are best thought of in an analytical process at the same time (Elvan and Tucker, 2015) and are therefore discussed simultaneously, below. Similarly, opportunities to enhance responses are often inhibited by the threats facing the IWT response, and so are also discussed jointly. The discussion continues with recommendations for addressing the deficiencies identified in the SWOT analysis.

Key Findings

The research findings suggest that the nature of the IWT in the UK and Norway is similar. Specifically, the type of animal victims, offender motivations and the nature of the marketplace are consistent: wildlife is used in the pet trade, and in the use of a wide range of luxury products and collector items. Both countries respond through international treaties and domestic legislation which support the enforcement, prosecution and judicial response. These responses are complex and diverse, necessitating multi-agency cooperation. A theme common to both locations was the importance of a small number of key personnel working together to prevent and respond to the trade; without them, responses would be seriously impaired. Deficiencies in both countries were evident, specifically linked with limited funding and prioritization within the criminal justice system. However, when responses were further evaluated, variations appeared in both practice and effectiveness.

These variations stem from the level of awareness of the serious negative consequences of the IWT, which directly impacts upon political and criminal justice system support for legislation, enforcement and punishment of offenders. The UK's multi-agency and specialized IWT enforcement response contrasts starkly with the insufficient Norwegian operation. The integrated role of NGOs in the UK enforcement process and in developing non-enforcement responses also contrasts with Norway, where NGO involvement is mostly absent. UK and Norwegian experts and practitioners alike argued that an effective response was one that was intelligence led, systematic, integrated and synergistic; they cited the importance of cooperation between enforcement agencies and NGOs and the necessity for increased prioritization of these crimes by criminal justice systems.

Swot Analysis

Strengths	***Weaknesses***
National legislation compliant with CITES Reptiles banned by legislation with a few exceptions (Norway) Classification of the IWT as a serious crime Specialist IWT enforcement agencies and officers and training for frontline staff (UK, Norway) Effective partnership work and communication between international enforcement agencies, including shared data systems at EU level (UK) Intelligence-led national IWT priorities (UK) Effective partnership work between enforcement and with non-enforcement agencies (UK) CITES proficiency at Environment(al) Agency NGOs central to the IWT response, providing intelligence, education, training and specialist advice and financial support (UK) Specialist facilities for the care of CITES wildlife (UK)	Incoherent/outdated domestic legislation (UK) Inconsistent application of laws and regulations Non-compliance and difficulty enforcing complicated CITES regulations (limited public and stakeholder awareness) Poor transparency in CITES cases through the CJS due to inconsistent coding in police and court files for all IWT offences Limited financial (and other) resources to enforce CITES Weakness in investigation, prosecution and sentencing of offences, with limited specialist training of agency staff Routine destruction of wildlife (Norway) and limited facilities for the care of wildlife
Opportunities	***Threats***
Revision of national and international legislation in line with current animal welfare requirements and controls for serious and organized crime Adoption of the ICCWC Wildlife and Forest Crime Analytical Toolkit Engagement with EU-TWIX as a central communication tool between EU enforcement agencies (and further development of similar systems beyond EU borders) Communication of 'Best Practice' in training, and enforcement to other EU Member States Engagement for all stakeholders through international and national fora/conferences Closer cooperation with NGOs to enhance IWT intelligence and responses The use and development of new enforcement techniques and technology Introduce restorative justice approach for victims	Porous country borders across EU (and other European) Member States Failure to establish common EU policies and enforcement practices (UK) Failure to prioritize the IWT, outward facing political interest and efforts (UK) Financial crisis – reductions in public budgets threatening specialist CJS agencies and intelligence gathering Failure of all EU enforcement agencies to engage with EU-TWIX The IWT perceived by offenders to be a high profit and low risk offence; offenses displaced rather than prevented Increased accessibility to vulnerable wildlife and expanding markets (growing cultural traditions and uses) and marketplaces (including online) fuelling the IWT Limited resources and responses when wildlife enters the trade

Strengths and Weaknesses

Legislation

Both countries have enacted CITES in national legislation. In Norway, breaches of the CITES regulation potentially incurs a maximum three-year prison sentence, depending on which law is applied (see above). Applied to their full potential, these laws could, hypothetically, have a deterrent effect. However, frequent use of the AWA (which prohibits the import and possession of exotic species) rather than CITES regulations, by the police and prosecutors, means these offences are not notifiable[23], thereby omitting would-be CITES cases from official statistics. This is particularly salient in hundreds of penal cases where an 'exotic species' is seized in relation to other crimes: classified only as 'animal welfare' offences, these animals cannot be confirmed as CITES species. Regardless of whether recognized as CITES or AWA (which also allows for up-to three years custody), offences are seldom brought to court. Without additional charges for 'more serious' offences, offenders commonly receive fines. These fines, also the norm in UK CITES cases, were criticized by interviewees on the basis that current legislation has provision for much tougher punishment. For example, CITES offences may fall under COTES (five years custody and/or an unlimited fine), CEMA (seven years custody and/or an unlimited fine), in national animal welfare/wildlife laws (e.g. AWA 2006 – a fine and/or six months custody) or breaches in EU regulations (e.g. (EC) No 1/2005 Animal Welfare in transportation – up to six months custody). Unsurprisingly, UK interviewees felt that these powers were a sufficient deterrent and punishment if used appropriately. However, concerns were raised over the timeliness of revisions to domestic legislation (COTES 1997 is only now under consultation for revision by DEFRA (2015)), the clarity of this legislation for enforcement purposes (domestic wildlife legislation is disjointed and incoherent) and the limited protection it confers to animals. Failure to revise and consolidate current legislation has produced fractures and loopholes and created barriers in the enforcement response. On the whole, animal welfare was deemed deficient in CITES legislation (UK and Norway). Consequently, in May 2015 the Norwegian Ministry of Climate and Environment received a suggested revision to the CITES regulations to strengthen the protection of CITES species from the Norwegian Environment Agency. In the UK, NGOs repeatedly highlighted penalties for killing or injuring wildlife as significantly lower than for incorrectly trading or paying duty on them. And even the incorporation of the International Air Transport Association [IATA][24] Live Animal Regulations

[LAR], as part of CITES compliance – which has reportedly simplified the prosecution for abuse linked to trafficking as 'suffering' need not be proved – is lessened by current EU Regulations that employ the old 2004 LAR standards (IATA, 2015).

Enforcement

The UK has recently prioritized the IWT as a serious crime, listing it as a key wildlife crime priority for the police. The Norwegian Police Directorate also identifies it as serious, prioritized crime. However, interviewees in both countries suggested that, in practice, it is treated like a minor crime, at all levels from detection to sentencing. It was also suggested that the lack of general awareness and compliance for IWT offences in Norway (and arguably in the UK) reflects this lack of prioritization by enforcement agencies and judicial systems alike. This is more surprising in the UK, where prioritization of the IWT has facilitated the development of specialized enforcement units, training for non-specialist enforcers, a commitment to the collection of intelligence and intelligence-led enforcement, and the development of partnership work with other enforcement agencies and key stakeholders. In contrast, the Norwegian enforcement response is generally characterized by little specialization (although specialized environmental crimes officers enforce CITES in police districts), training or multi-agency cooperation.

IWT offence data in both countries is limited and interviewees argued that it is feasible that recorded offences present a very small percentage of the actual IWT. Disappointingly, despite being recognized for stringent record keeping, databases tracking IWT offences are conspicuous by their absence in Norway. Norwegian customs do record their seizures, though CITES offences are not categorized according to substance (Toll, 2013)[25], nor do they appear in public statistics (see seizure statistics for 2014, Toll, 2014). Additionally, interviewees (from both locations) recognized that some IWT offences go undetected because non-specialist officers (in customs or the police) have significant difficulty working with a complicated and ever-changing list of illegal species, and because enforcement agencies have not set CITES seizure targets. Many CITES offences surface, more or less, by accident or in conjunction with more 'serious' offences such as drug, alcohol and/or tobacco smuggling (for which there are set seizure targets). The UK customs agency also records CITES offences, details of which are published in greater detail online than those available in Norway (Data.gov.uk, 2015). Courtesy of the development of the specialized police National Wildlife Crime Unit (NWCU), further data is collected from all police forces nationwide, providing intelligence for setting UK wildlife enforcement priorities and developing a risk-based targeted enforcement approach. Despite these positives, many police forces do not return the necessary information to the NWCU. And whilst most UK officers are not trained to identify CITES products, the UK CITES customs team provide training for enforcement personnel, and has raised the profile of IWT offences, resulting in better understanding and detection among all enforcement officers. These specialized CITES enforcement teams have been responsible for significant increases in seizures and arrests. It is likely that setting clear targets (for customs), albeit very low ones, has contributed to their success.

UK interviewees unanimously regarded the development of successful partnerships between enforcement agencies and with NGOs and other stakeholders as crucial to a successful enforcement response. NCA officers, who hold combined enforcement powers and may arrest, search, seize, acquire information and recover criminal assets, provide customs and NWCU with stronger enforcement capabilities and a more fluid and robust response. This development of specialized teams and partnership work is linked to optimum or targeted enforcement (maximum impact with limited resources). And yet, while these teams are small, they frequently experience funding crises. Consequently, NGOs have campaigned relentlessly to raise political awareness and funding, and have even directly funded enforcement agencies. In 2012, World Animal Protection provided funding to prevent the Metropolitan Wildlife Crime Unit from closing, and there after analyzed and published seizure data and provided forensic toolkits (new technologies offer significant opportunities for the enforcement of IWT). As with other forged links between UK NGOs and enforcement agencies there has been successful cooperation, including targeted operations (e.g. Operation Charm), data-sharing, and increased public education and awareness. These successes, however, highlight the lack of financial and political support for the enforcement response (which would be compromised without NGO support). Outside of the specialized IWT teams, there is also a notable absence of resources; enforcement officers with partial IWT responsibilities reported their IWT duties were de-prioritized or carried out outside working hours. Resource issues were also noted in Norway, where customs officers complained they were refused the Green Parrot computer program which facilitates easy identification of CITES offences (through listing species and certificates). Here, as mentioned, CITES cases are usually left to environmental crime officers in each police district, though, with heavy workloads, these officers struggle to prioritize this work. With funding clearly limited in both countries, and resources for CITES enforcement scarce, the wealth of knowledge, expertise and networks established by a few persons has, undoubtedly, been crucial to the control and enforcement of CITES offences.

Prosecution and Punishment

The prosecution and sentencing of IWT offenders was perceived, by most interviewees in both locations, to be the weakest link in the criminal justice response. Prosecution rates were described as very poor and a consequence of the limited experience and expertise in the Crown Prosecution Service (CPS) and Judiciary. Central to this problem, was the lack of accountability (e.g. cases are not consistently coded or traceable through the CJS) and specialist training (with the exception of Scotland in the UK) for these agencies. While UK enforcement officers detailed partnership work with the CPS which resulted in successful prosecutions and suitable punishment, there were many more occasions where a robust case was ineffectively prosecuted, if at all. There were also examples where Norwegian state prosecutors produced insufficient cases (without using former cases as precedence) resulting in only lenient punishment for the offenders. Prosecutions in both locations also failed because of long delays in the prosecution process. Successful prosecutions in both locations were characterized by inconsistency in the application of sanctions and incongruence between sanctions and the severity of the offence. For example, in 2012 an offender was fined 10,000 NOK for importing 25 CITES listed parrots into Norway, while in 1998 the most punitive sentence to date – four months custody – was passed for a CITES offence involving a prolific offender who had on 20 occasions smuggled over 200 birds (many CITES I and II listed parrots) into Norway. These sentences are lenient, inadequately protect endangered species, and unlikely to deter would-be offenders motivated by typically vast financial rewards. Similarly, political and governmental commitment and prioritization is at odds with the requirements of effective enforcement and sentencing. In the UK, according to NGO interviewees, this is due to the outward-facing (e.g. international) nature of the UK political IWT agenda. However, enforcement interviewees argued this was a consequence of limited joined-up intelligence and competing priorities with other more serious crimes.

Welfare

The purpose of CITES is to ensure wildlife trade is sustainable, to enable future exploitation, it is not intended to protect individual animals. Within this framework, protection for individual animals is therefore limited at best. Interviewees provided many examples of the poor conditions in which trafficked animals arrived in the UK and Norway. Interestingly, while Norway generally bans trade and possession of reptiles, UK interviewees expressed particular concern over the welfare impact on exotic animals, identifying this pet trade as one of its most pressing concerns. For example, CITES reptiles are laundered as part of the legal trade, smuggled in overcrowded, often lethal conditions contradictory to requirements in the IATA LAR. Should an airline (which is responsible for ensuring customers fulfil requirements) breach the IATA regulations, it may be refused a license to import live animals. However, as a UK vet explained, there is no database of such breaches across EU Member States, without which prior offences cannot be identified and airlines can easily breach regulations in multiple locations.

While animal welfare is not of central concern in CITES, Member States are required to provide for the welfare of confiscated and seized wildlife. Through the purpose-built UK Heathrow ARC, all confiscated/ seized wildlife are appropriately housed and re-homed. However, due to delays in prosecution and/or re-homing, some animals are required to remain at the ARC for long periods in what should be temporary accommodation. While few animals are returned to the wild, interviewees nonetheless said the rehoming process was successful due to close cooperation between agencies and interest groups (e.g. zoos and sanctuaries). With limited capacity and insufficient monitoring of re-homing locations, these informal arrangements are a cause for concern. With no legal requirement – COTES does not stipulate rehoming requirements for seized wildlife – it is left to committed agency staff to facilitate these arrangements. In Norway, the continued victimization of seized animals was well documented, with euthanasia the rule rather than the exception. The only exception remains when Kristiansand Zoo and Oslo Reptile Park agreed to receive seized animals. Although the Norwegian Environment Agency states the goal is to return confiscated CITES animals to where they belong, analysis of verdicts showed that confiscation (and subsequent euthanasia) may be argued for (by the judge) in order to fulfil Norway's obligation to CITES. For example, when a Norwegian man with CITES permits for 36 birds imported 44, the surplus birds were killed by the authorities. Given that the Norwegian CITES regulations only attend to welfare in paragraph 16, this should be unsurprising:

'If import of a specimen which is already in the country cannot be permitted, the Norwegian Environment Agency shall ensure the specimen is taken care of…Living individuals can be returned after demand from the conservation authorities in the exporting state. The costs in relation to such shipments shall be covered by the exporting state. The shipment must take place in a way that does not cause the individual harm or unnecessary suffering' (Author's translation and emphasis). 'Welfare' appears to be the 'Achilles' heel of much IWT practice, leaving a great deal to be desired in effectively responding to the trade.

Opportunities and Threats Legislation

The UK has identified the need to revise key legislation relating to CITES, a process currently underway in Norway. There is an opportunity in the UK to use research evidence and consultation (e.g. UK Environmental Audit Committee 2012) to enhance prevention, enforcement and sentencing of IWT offences and prioritize the animal victims within legislation. One of the greatest challenges facing the UK is failure among fellow EU Member States to further develop their legislation; failure to develop common domestic IWT policy provides loopholes that UK offenders will continue to exploit. The development of organized criminal networks in the IWT also poses new challenges for UK and Norwegian authorities and requires new legislative tools for enforcement and prosecution. There is, though, an opportunity to take example from the enforcement of other serious and organized crimes to help deliver more robust legislation. For example, an IWT case awaiting trial in Norway is using §60 in the Norwegian Penal Law (the so-called 'Mafia/organised crime' paragraph) – which has been employed successfully in an illegal wolf killing case. The Norwegian reptile ban is also worth noting – while it has not succeeded in preventing reptiles from entering the country, it makes control of endangered reptile species easier to enforce. Specifically, specialized knowledge to differentiate species is not required and it changes the market for these species as it deters people from purchasing one on a whim (which is sadly often the case for parrots, which are legal). This suggests that a ban on all IWT could improve enforcement responses.

Enforcement, Prosecution and Punishment

There is considerable variation in the priority given to regulating and enforcing the IWT across EU and partnership countries, thus, the most serious threat to enforcement responses are porous borders. Once illegal wildlife/products enter one EU Member State, it becomes more difficult for other enforcement agencies to identify and apprehend offenders. The prioritization given to the IWT at government level is central to this issue; however, as demonstrated by the UK enforcement funding crisis (which has caused uncertainty and reduced efficiency and effectiveness), this prioritization must be focused internally and externally. When political will is low, as is the case in Norway, this threatens awareness among enforcement and sentencing agencies, stakeholders, and the general public (at a time when wildlife products are easier to obtain than ever before). The IWT is not primarily a source country problem – there would be no IWT market without the demand from wealthy EU and other countries. Furthermore, the prioritization of other serious crimes (e.g. drug trafficking) by the CJS threatens the IWT response. Evidence suggests that offenders may be displaced from one crime to another and the IWT is increasingly recognized as a high profit, low risk offence – it is sure to attract offenders. Continued activity amongst organized crime networks is also a significant threat; current enforcement responses are not nearly robust enough to respond effectively. UK enforcement interviewees, for example, stated that they were unable to follow-up on IWT leads to organized crime due to limited resources and because set targets had already been exceeded. Current developments in enforcement techniques and technology–including DNA databases, forensic analysis, sniffer dogs, IT software/hardware and UAVs – provide opportunities for improving enforcement capacity, while reducing costs. While there is limited use of these in both locations, UK evidence suggests these are essential to a successful enforcement response.

Significantly, the UK and Norway already produce detailed data and analysis, from seizure, arrest, and prosecution to the sentencing of offenders, for other serious crimes. It seems reasonable to suggest that these processes be adopted and applied to the IWT. Equally, legislation and policy used to respond to other serious international crimes could be adopted by all Member States in response to the IWT. The ICCWC Wildlife and Forest Crime Analytical Toolkit is freely available to Member States, though it is not currently utilized in either location. Even so, this resource presents opportunities to strengthen existing enforcement processes and identify alternative approaches. Norway could take advantage of its highly educated police organization (three years at university college level, in addition to a MA program) - CITES training could become standard for police students, promoting competence in front-line staff which would reduce the pressure on overworked specialized environment officers. CITES training (theory and practice) could also fit into customs officers training (who complete a 26 month training program). Likewise, opportunities to embed CITES should be investigated in the UK. As a minimum, it should be rooted in police and customs training.

Perhaps the greatest opportunity to improve the enforcement response in both countries lies in increased communication and cooperation, both nationally and internationally, between enforcement agencies and key stakeholders. Utilizing established communication tools (e.g. EU-TWIX – an online forum and database developed by the Belgian Federal Police to assist national law enforcement agencies across the EU, including CITES Management Authorities and prosecutors, in their task of detecting, analyzing and monitoring WLT activities) and international fora (e.g. World Customs Organization [WCO], CITES CoP, Interpol, UN, EU) could help expand opportunities to cooperate and share 'best practice' and specialized training and knowledge. The UK CITES customs team are developing an international reputation for their specialized IWT training and assistance to enforcement officers around the world. Their efforts secure future cooperation, partnership and a unified IWT enforcement approach. Enforcement operations involving the UK and Norway, such as Operations Tramp and Charm, have demonstrated the value and effectiveness of international cooperation and communication. Nonetheless, Norwegian enforcement agencies need to engage further with established fora developed for enforcement agencies. It was also identified that communication between international enforcement agencies is limited by data confidentiality (and trust).More positively, EU TWIX, as an example, was described by UK interviewees as an essential 'closed' enforcement tool for communication, enabling swift exchange of information/intelligence between Member States. However, engagement with EU TWIX seemingly varies considerably from one country to another and its effectiveness is largely dependent on regular inputs from all Member States.

Welfare

It is increasingly necessary to secure improvements in the welfare of animal victims of the IWT, and engagement with NGOs provides a key opportunity for CJS agencies to do so. NGOs such as WAP, WWF, and IFAW can share expertise on welfare requirements, awareness campaigns and prevention and intervention strategies with offenders and their communities. Failure to reduce the demand for animals and animal products is a significant threat to a successful response to the IWT, but the greatest threat must be the failure to protect and keep wildlife in the wild: with few exceptions, once an animal is removed from its home, it never returns.

Recommendations: Actions towards Preventing/Eliminating the Trade

From the SWOT analysis, a portfolio of actions can be inferred, some linked to strengths and weaknesses, while others capitalize on opportunities and counteract threats. In suggesting the following recommendations, we have considered those we deem to be the most viable. However, we are aware that not all of the opportunities we detail here are realistic, perhaps because of political, economic or other external dimensions, but as researchers hoping our work can improve the lot of animal victims, we have included these ideas. And while this case study focused on two countries, the strengths and deficiencies discussed here are unlikely to be limited to these; identified weaknesses in the control and enforcement of the IWT are applicable outside of the UK and Norway (for example, punishment was also lenient in Columbia and Brazil). Our recommendations include a non-speciesist approach (Beirne, 1999) and fall into three broad categories: legislation, enforcement, prosecution and punishment, and welfare.

Legislation

The nature of the IWT ensures that animal victims suffer significant harms – both in terms of individual harms and to animal species as a whole. This breaches their individual interests and species and ecological justice (cf. White, 2013).We recommend the harmonization of legislation, to modernize and improve current enforcement, and also the embedding of animals' welfare into legislative systems for the control of the IWT. Speciesism is doxic, meaning that practices that exploit animals are taken for granted by the great majority (Sollund, 2012). The fact that the wildlife trade is both legal and illegal makes it difficult to convey a strong normative message through the application of laws and regulations. Rather, the message which is conveyed by CITES as well as the enforcement approach is mixed– the IWT may be legally wrong but is morally right. The central point, that animals are sentient beings, is constantly under-communicated if not totally neglected. While a total ban would convey a stronger message to offenders, it is unlikely to happen due to the economic value of the trade. In any case, the governing anthropocentrism and speciesism evident in the CJS would significantly limit the enforcement of a ban. Furthermore, bans may increase the value of endangered species and thereby increase profits for the IWT (Rivalan et al., 2007; Low in Sollund, 2011).

While we understand the difficulty in doing so, we argue that CITES (and parties to CITES), acknowledging current research into the cognitive skills and properties of nonhuman animals (see Pepperberg, 2009 regarding African Grey parrots), recognize that the current exploitative regime of sentient beings should not be morally or legally supported. As a move towards this, we propose thatMember States review domestic legislation in order to respond to current IWT issues (e.g. organized crime) and to further embed animal welfare. Also, that the EU update the Council Regulation (EC) No 1/2005 in line with the enhanced welfare standards set out in the IATA LAR 2015 as part of CITES compliance and that Member States be required to report IATA LAR transgressions by airlines, to the Traces system (used for re-entry documents), to make transport companies accountable for their actions and to prevent future infringements.

Enforcement, Prosecution and Punishment

In order to conduct an audit for funding and resource management for the IWT, both Norway and the UK (and CITES members) should be encouraged to utilize the ICCWC Wildlife and Forest Crime Analytic Toolkit and engage with (or adopt something similar to) the EU-TWIX database. Since one important finding from this case study is that serious crimes (e.g. drugs) are prioritized by the CJS, at the cost of detection and enforcement of the IWT, and this may in turn cause organized criminals to concentrate on the IWT, similar targets as those set for drugs should be set for IWT offences. However, in doing so, it is important to take a proportional overview of resources for other serious offences and to set targets which measure the right thing. To enhance accountability and detection, and to avoiddysfunction (e.g. practices to corrupt figures), these targets need careful consideration. Linked to this is the inconsistent coding of IWT offences, which increases the 'dark' figure of the IWT and prevents accountability in the judicial system. Therefore, it is recommended that all IWT cases are notifiable offences and uniquely coded through the CJS to establish a more accurate picture of the nature and prevalence of the trade.

Partnership work and cooperation between CJS agencies and with NGOs and stakeholders are showing promising results in the UK, as is international cooperation. We therefore propose that Norway (and all CITES members) develop an enforcement response focusing on multi-agency cooperation and communication both nationally and internationally. A key finding in the case study was the limitations in the enforcement response resulting from a lack of specialization and general training of front line staff. Therefore, CITES training should be embedded in the training of all front line officers, and should become a specialization for a smaller number in the customs and police. Countries are advised to use the resources currently available across Member States (e.g. UK CITES team training) in order to do so. More urgently, specialized training and guidance is required for the CPS and judiciary to ensure CITES cases are supported and prosecuted consistently and appropriately, using the full weight of the law.

In arguing for this, we acknowledge that a punitive response is not necessarily the best approach to dealing with all CITES offences.

Whether a punishment will have a deterrent effect would depend on what the offenders gain from their involvement in the IWT, and what they lose by abstaining from it. It is well documented that motivations for offending vary depending on the role of the offender in the chain, from poaching to consumption. Therefore, to support the enforcement approach, we advocate that education and awareness strategies to reduce consumer demand for IWT health and beauty products, luxury foods and pets are utilized across the EU and Norway (with support from NGOs). This is especially important in the case of wildlife products whereby most of the consumption is not necessary in any legitimizing way, but is instead determined by cravings for luxury goods. While failure in enforcement and punishment may limit deterrence from the IWT, the majority of potential offenders in relation to most crimes normally offend due to ignorance of legislation (Aubert, 1954). Thus, consumers in receiver countries may potentially be deterred by a heightened risk of punishment. In order for legislation to have a preventative impact, certainty of punishment is more important than severity; interviewees suggest that in the best cases there is some attention to severity and in the worst, both certainty and severity are absent.

While this article has focused on the IWT response in predominantly receiver and transit countries, we also acknowledge that these recommendations may be useful in source countries where financial aid could help to develop a more robust enforcement and judicial response. Awareness campaigns are also essential to prevent the trade at the most vital point – when animals are removed from the wild. Considering the developments in the organized IWT, arguments could be made for UN troop support for local wildlife rangers who are confronted with armed, organised poacher groups.

Welfare

While the focus on the consequences of the trade is generally anthropocentric, regarding the loss of animal species to be mainly a human problem, it is necessary to expand this perspective to include the innumerable animals that are victimized due to trafficking and the environmental costs to ecosystems. Therefore, as a matter of urgency, the EU (and CITES parties) should clarify their position in relation to the responsibilities toward confiscated/seized live animals and require transparency from all Member States by way of an annual report on the outcomes for all seized wildlife.

In doing so, all Member States should make a formal commitment to protect seized/confiscated wildlife and to provide sufficient funding to ensure their welfare (e.g. suitable long-term accommodation, provision for short-term accommodation at key locations). CITES states in Resolution Conf. 9.10 (Rev. CoP15) that when the Scientific Authority of the confiscating state deems it in the interest of the animal (specimen) to be returned, then such costs, and also costs in relation to custody and destruction of the animal, shall be claimed from the trafficker. One should assume that repatriation, rather than destruction, would be in the best interest of the animal, and therefore there is a strong case for exploring the use of a restorative justice approach to the IWT. While euthanasia is incompatible with taking care of wildlife, from an anthropocentric viewpoint, Norway is actually fulfilling its obligations towards CITES. From a species justice viewpoint, killing them is morally unjust and it is hard to see how this practice may serve to protect endangered species. Additionally, while unnecessary suffering (but from whose perspective?) is the criteria upon which to judge what is to be done with wildlife, very little protection is offered to individual animal trafficking victims. This issue is highlighted in most animal welfare legislation, where the expression 'unnecessary suffering' is also frequently and controversially applied (e.g. Francione, 2007; Beirne, 2009; Kleveland, 2013).

Both the UK and Norwegian enforcement agencies raise awareness of the IWT through their websites (e.g. NWCU) and specialist magazines (e.g. Miljøkrim published by the Norwegian Eco-crime unit), but also by means of press releases to daily newspapers and television. In responding to the IWT, it is essential to further raise public and stakeholder awareness of the consequences of the IWT (e.g. for the animal victims) through better data collection and reporting (by police, customs, or government departments)via press releases detailing seizure/confiscation rates, the treatment of wildlife, and potential and actual punishments received by offenders.

Conclusion

Despite growing concern, international political will and promises of eradication, the IWT is increasing. It may in future outstrip other illicit enterprises in terms of its multifarious nature and the complexities it poses for control and law enforcement. This article has provided further understanding of these challenges by evaluating data from a multi-method qualitative case study on the IWT in two countries. Drawing from the UK and Norway, a comparison is made through the lens of a SWOT analysis and evaluation of these findings through a green criminology harms perspective. As parties to CITES, and key marketplaces for the IWT, both countries have a responsibility to provide a robust response. Unfortunately, SWOT analysis identifies that while responses are similar, approaches and practices vary, and give rise to varying levels of ineffectiveness. The UK, in particular, does demonstrate strengths in their legislation, enforcement and care of the wildlife, but the response, in both countries, suffers from a general lack of awareness and prioritization, limited resources, unsuccessful prosecutions and inadequate penalties. Consequently, risk of detection is low and punishment uncertain, resulting in moderate enforcement which fails to act as a general or individual deterrent. Accordingly, the IWT is likely to increase, facilitated as it is by globalization and capitalization. Unacceptably, due to the limited protection conferred to the wildlife caught by the trade and the limited facilities for receiving wildlife in the UK and Norway, a steadily increasing number of animals are likely to be harmed and killed.

The recommendations highlighted by the SWOT findings are for the short and long-term. Short-term, the key recommendations are: harmonization of regulations and enforcement practices in Member States; provision of specialist IWT training for all CJS agencies; commitment to the use of EU-TWIX and application of existing tools such as the ICCWC Wildlife and Forest Crime Analytic Toolkit; augmentation of animal welfare through CITES policy (for seized/confiscated wildlife) and legislation (e.g. IATA LAR, 2015); prioritization of CITES and application of the full punishment threshold provided in law; and further development of prevention and intervention responses. Long-term, in line with green criminology's victimology and species and ecological justice perspectives (White, 2013), it is recommended that there is a move towards the acknowledgement of nonhuman animals as victims of trafficking, as having equal capacity to suffer from harms such as deprivation of freedom, peers, offspring and adequate nutrition, and because the IWT, like human trafficking, involves enslavement, harm and frequently death (Sollund, 2013b).

Notes

1. TRAFFIC is the leading global NGO wildlife trade monitoring network: www.traffic.org.
2. CITES, a voluntary international agreement between governments
3. Colombia and Brazil are omitted in this analysis due to space limitations.
4. SWOT is widely adopted in academic research, public administration and policy development throughout Europe, used to select policy, priorities and ensure

horizontal policy coherence in their national strategies for sustainable development (Markoska et al. 2009).

5. Also Council Regulation (EC) No. 865/2006, which constitute the legal framework for WT for EU Member States: http://eur-lex.europa.eu/LexUriServ/LexUriServ.do?uri=CELEX:31997R0338:EN:HTML
6. http://www.legislation.gov.uk/uksi/1997/1421/contents/madeand
7. http://www.legislation.gov.uk/uksi/1997/1372/contents/made
8. http://www.legislation.gov.uk/ukpga/1979/2
9. http://www.legislation.gov.uk/ukpga/2006/45/contents
10. http://www.legislation.gov.uk/ukpga/1981/69/contents
11. http://www.legislation.gov.uk/ukpga/1984/60/contents
12. https://lovdata.no/dokument/SF/forskrift/2002-11-15-1276
13. http://lovdata.no/dokument/NL/lov/2009-06-19-100
14. http://lovdata.no/dokument/NL/lov/1981-05-29-38 (Revised 2009).
15. http://lovdata.no/dokument/NL/lov/1997-06-06-32
16 https://lovdata.no/dokument/NL/lov/1925-07-17-11/KAPITTEL 1 # KAPITTEL 1.
17. https://lovdata.no/dokument/NL/lov/1930-02-27-2/%C2%A72#§2
18. http://lovdata.no/dokument/NL/lov/2009-06-19-97
19. http://lovdata.no/dokument/SF/forskrift/1976-11-20-3
20. Statistics provided upon request.
21. Norwegian data also included 87 penal cases coded as (2510): Illegal importation of alien wildlife species (under the Wildlife law § 47) and 723 penal cases coded as (5901) Illegal importation/dealing with exotic species § 30 nr.76 (Under the animal welfare act), by the police.
22. This research was conducted in accordance with the ethical guidance of the EC, British Society of Criminology, University of South Wales, the Norwegian Social Science Data Services and NESH (The Norwegian National Research Ethics Committees).
23. An offence for which the police must complete a crime report for statistical purposes.
24. Trade association for 250 airlines, help formulate aviation policy, including setting the minimum welfare standards for the transportation of animals
25. CITES seizures registered as fauna here, most likely include flora.

References

Aubert, V. (1954). *Om straffens sosiale funksjon*. Akademiskforlag.

Baillie, J., Hilton-Taylor, C. & Stuart, S. (Eds.). (2004). *2004 IUCN red list of threatened species: A global species assessment*. Cambridge: International Union for Conservation of Nature.

Beirne, P. (1999). For a non-speciesist criminology: Animal abuse as an object of study. *Criminology*, 37(1):117-148.

Beirne, P. (2009). *Confronting animal abuse: Law, criminology, and human-animal relationships*. Maryland: Rowman & Littlefield Publishers.

Beirne, P. & South, N. (2007). Introduction to green criminology. In Beirne, P. and South, N. (Eds.), *Issues in green criminology*. Devon: Willan.

Cao, A.G. & Wyatt, T. (2013). A Green Criminological Exploration of Illegal Wildlife Trade in Vietnam. *Asian Journal of Criminology*, 8(2): 129-142.

Convention on International Trade in Endangered Species of Wild Fauna and Flora [CITES] (2013). *Heads of UNODC and CITES urge wildlife and forest offences to be treated as serious transnational organized crimes*. Retrieved from http://www.cites.org/eng/news/pr/2013/20130423 CCPCJ.php.

CITES (2014).*The CITES species*. Retrieved from http://www.cites.org/eng/disc/species.php.

Dealtry T. R. (1992). *Dynamic SWOT analysis: Developer's guide*. Birmingham: Dynamic SWOT Associates.

Department for Environment, Food and Rural Affairs (2015). *Consultation on proposed changes to the control of trade in endangered species regulations*. Retrieved from https://consult.defra.gov.uk/biodiversity/changing-cotes-regulations/supporting documents/COTES % 20 Review % 20 % 20 Consultation % 20 Document. pdf.

Data.gov.uk. (2015). *Convention on international trade in endangered species (CITES) seizures and volumes*. Retrieved from http://data.gov.uk/dataset/convention-on-international-trade-in-endangered-species-cites-seizures-and-volumes/resource/334c3200-324f-4e51-b51d-b4f287908177.

Duffy, R. (2010). *Nature crime: how we are getting conservation wrong*. New Haven: Yale University Press.

Elvan, O. D. & Turker, Y. O. (2015). Access to justice in environmental matters in Turkey: A case study from the ancient city of Allianoi. *International Journal of Law, Crime and Justice*, 43(4): 424-438.

European Commission (2014). *Communication from the commission to the council and the European parliament on the EU approach against wildlife trafficking*. Brussels: European Commission.

Europol (2011). *European organised crime groups active in trafficking endangered species*. Retrieved from https://www.europol.europa.eu/content/press/european-organised-crime-groups-active-trafficking-endangered-species-425.

Europol (2013). *Threat assessment 2013 environmental crime in the EU*. Retrieved from: https://www.europol.europa.eu/.../4 aenvironmental crime threatassessm ... % 20 Cached % 20Similar.

Fitzgerald, A. J. (2010). The underdog as ideal victim? The attribution of victimhood in the 2007 Pet food recall. *International Review of Victimology*, 17:131-157.

Francione, G. L. (2007). Reflections on Animals, Property, and the Law and Rain without Thunder. *Law and Contemporary Problems*, 70:9-57.

Glaser, B., & Strauss, A. (1967). *The discovery of grounded theory: Strategies for qualitative research*. Chicago: Aldine Publishing Company

International Air Transport Association (2015). *Live animal regulations manual*. Retrieved from http://www.labeline.com/store uk/ecom-prodshow/iata live animal regulations 41st 2015.html.

International Fund for Animal Welfare. (2008). *Killing with keystrokes. An investigation of the Illegal wildlife trade on the world wide web*. Retrieved from http://www.ifaw.org/Publications/Program Publications/Wildlife Trade/ Campaign Scientific Publications/asset upload file64 12456.pdf.

Interpol and International Fund for Animal Welfare (2013). *Project web: An investigation into the ivory trade over the internet within the European Union*. Environmental Crime Program. Interpol.

Kleveland, L. (2013). Livet, smerten og friheten. Sikres dyrs interesser av dyrevelferd-sloven og forvaltningen In Sollund, R. et al. (Eds.), *Hvemervillest I landet her? Råskap mot dyrogmennesker I anropocen, mennesketstidsalder*. Oslo Spartacaus SAP.

Lavorgna, A. (2014). Wildlife trafficking in the Internet age. *Crime Science*, 3(1):1-12.

Lawson, K., & Vines, A. (2014). *Global impacts of the illegal wildlife trade: The costs of crime, insecurity and institutional erosion*. UK: Chatham House.

Markovska, N. Taseska, V. & Pop-Jordanov, J. (2009). SWOT analyses of the national energy sector for sustainable energy development. *Energy*, 34(6): 752-756.

Nibert, D. (2002). *Animal rights/human rights: Entanglements of oppression and liberation*. Maryland: Rowman & Littlefield Publishers.

Pepperberg, I. M. (2009). *The Alex studies: cognitive and communicative abilities of grey parrots*. Harvard University Press.

Regan, T. (1983). *The case for animal rights*. Berkley: University of California Press.

Reeve, R. (2002). *Policing international trade in endangered species: The CITES treaty and compliance*. London: Earthscan.

Royal Society for the Prevention of Cruelty to Animals (n.d.). *Far from home – reptiles that suffer and die in captivity*. Retrieved from www.rspca.org.uk/.../Locate Asset % 3Fasset=document

Rivalan, P. et al.(2007). Can bans stimulate wildlife trade? *Nature*, 447:529-530.

Schneider, J. (2012). *Sold into extinction: The global trade in endangered species*. Santa Barbara: Praeger.

Sollund, R. (2011). Expressions of speciesism: the effects of keeping companion animals on animal abuse, animal trafficking and species decline. *Crime, Law and Social Change*, 55(5): 437-451.

Sollund, R. (2012). Speciesism as doxic practice versus valuing difference and plurality. In Ellefsen, R, et al. (Eds.), *Eco-global crimes. Contemporary problems and future challenges*. Farnham: Ashgate Publishing.

Sollund, R. (2013a). Animal trafficking and trade: Abuse and species injustice. In D. Westerhuis et al. (Eds.), *Emerging issues in green criminology: exploring power, justice and harm*. London: Palgrave.

Sollund, R. (2013b). The victimization of women, children and nonhuman species through trafficking and trade. Crimes understood through an Ecofeminist perspective. In South, N. and Brisman, A. (Eds), *The Routledge Handbook in Green Criminology*. London: Routledge.

Sollund, R., & Maher, J. (2015). *Illegal wildlife trade: A case study report on the illegal wildlife trade in the United Kingdom, Norway, Colombia and Brazil*.

Retrieved from http://efface.eu/illegal-wildlife-trade-case-study-report-illegal-wildlife-trade-united-kingdom-norway-colombia-and#overlay-context=case-studies.

South, N., & Wyatt, T. (2011). Comparing illicit trades in wildlife and drugs: an exploratory study. *Deviant Behavior*, 32(6): 538-561.

Stretesky, P. B., Long, M. A. & Lynch. M. J. (2013). *The treadmill of crime: Political economy and green criminology*. London: Routledge.

Svae-Grotli, I. (2014). En forbrytelse å la alvorlig miljøkriminalitet forbli forseelser. *Miljøkrim* 1:30-36.

Toll (2013). *Beslagsstatistikk 2013: Seizurestatistics 2013*. Retrieved from https://www.toll.no/no/arkiv/beslagsstatistikk-for-2013/

Toll (2014). *Beslagsstatistikk 2014: Seizure statistics 2014*. Retrieved from http://www. toll. no/no/felles/om-tollvesenet/statistikk/beslagsstatistikk1/beslag sstatistikk - 2014/.

TRAFFIC (2008). *What's driving the wildlife trade? A review of expert opinion on economic and social drivers of the wildlife trade and trade control efforts in Cambodia, Indonesia, Lao PDR and Vietnam*. Retrieved from http://siteresources.worldbank. org/ INTEASTASIAPACIFIC/ Resources/226262-1223319129600/ wildlife foreword terms acknowledgement. pdf.

UNODC (2012). *Wildlife and forest crime analytic toolkit revised edition*. Vienna: United Nations.

UNODC (2013). *Heads of UNODC and CITES urge wildlife and forest offences to be treated as serious transnational organized crimes*. Retrieved from http://www.unodc.org/unodc/en/frontpage/2013/April/heads-of-unodc-and-cites-urge-wildlife-and-forest-offences-to-be-treated-as-serious-transnational-organized-crimes.htmlb.

van Uhm, D. (2014).Illegal wildlife trade to the EU and harms to the world. In Spapens, T. White, R. and. Huisman, W. (Eds.). *Environmental crime and the world*. London: Ashgate.

Warchol, G., Zupan, L., & Clarke W. (2003). Transnational criminality: An analysis of the illegal wildlife market in Southern Africa. *International Criminal Justice Review*, 13(1):1-26.

White, R. (2013). *Environmental harm* Bristol: Policy Press.

Wyatt, T. (2009). Exploring the organization in Russia Far East's illegal wildlife trade. Two case studies of the illegal fur and illegal falcon trades. *Global Crime*, 10 (1&2): 144-154.

Wyatt, T. (2011). Illegal raptor trade in the Russian federation. *Contemporary Justice Review*, 14 (2):103-123.

Wyatt, T. (2013). *Wildlife trafficking: A deconstruction of the crime, the victims, and the offenders*. London: Palgrave Macmillan.

Index